TWELFTH NIGHT
BY WILLIAM SHAKESPEARE

Edited by

GEORGE LYMAN KITTREDGE

GINN AND COMPANY
BOSTON · NEW YORK · CHICAGO
LONDON · ATLANTA · DALLAS · COLUMBUS · SAN FRANCISCO

𝕿𝖍𝖊 𝕬𝖙𝖍𝖊𝖓𝖆𝖚𝖒 𝕻𝖗𝖊𝖘𝖘

GINN AND COMPANY · PRO-
PRIETORS · BOSTON · U.S.A.

PREFACE

THE text is complete and agrees with that in Kittredge's edition of Shakespeare's *Works*. The numbering of the lines accords with that commonly used in citing the plays. This method is preferred to a new counting in order to facilitate reference to such standard works as Bartlett's *Concordance* and Schmidt's *Shakespeare-Lexicon*. In prose passages there results some slight irregularity in computation, but this does not indicate any omission in the text.

G. L. K.

CONTENTS

CONTENTS

INTRODUCTION

The text of TWELFTH NIGHT, as printed in the Folio of 1623, is unusually accurate. There is no earlier edition.

John Manningham of the Middle Temple saw TWELFTH NIGHT performed on February 2, 1602. 'At our feast,' he notes in his *Diary*, 'wee had a play called Twelue Night, or What You Will, much like the Commedy of Errores, or Menechmi in Plautus, but most like and neere to that in Italian called *Inganni*.' He commends particularly the trick played on Malvolio, which he calls 'a good practise' (i. e., a clever device). 'Twelue' is an old form of the ordinal; the Folio spells it 'twelfe.' Manningham's record fixes one limit for the date of composition. Obviously he had never seen the play before, but that does not prove that it was absolutely new. The title tempts inference that the first production was on the twelfth night (Epiphany) immediately preceding, that is, on January 6, 1602. Anyhow, 1601 (or 1600 at the earliest) may safely be accepted as the date of composition. No circumstantial evidence conflicts with this date. 'The new map with the augmentation of the Indies' (iii, 2, 85) was doubtless that of Emerie Molyneux (*ca.* 1599). The 'pension of thousands to be paid from the Sophy' (ii, 5, 197), that is, the Shah of Persia, may allude to Sir Robert Shirley's return from that country in 1599, with rich gifts from the Shah. Support for the accepted date (1600 or 1601) has been sought in Ben Jonson's *Poetaster* (iii, 4), where Captain Tucca describes a certain 'fat fool' called Mango. The passage has been thought to glance at Sir Toby Belch. *Poetaster* was acted in 1601. The evidence would be welcome if it were trustworthy, but Tucca's Mango never could have played Sir Toby.

The source for the main plot of TWELFTH NIGHT is Barnabe Riche's tale *Of Apolonius and Silla*, the second 'historie' in *Riche his Farewell to Militarie Profession* (1581).

Shakespeare's Viola is Riche's Silla. Viola's romance begins with a shipwreck, which separated her from her brother Sebastian and cast her up on
Duke Orsino's Illyrian coast. Silla is likewise shipwrecked, but the first
chapter of her love story is staged in Cyprus, at her father's court, where she
fell in love with Duke Apolonius, her father's guest, and sought to win him,
but in vain. Apolonius returns to his home in Constantinople and Silla
determines to follow him. The shipwreck is the end of her journey. Her
brother Silvio is not with her, but she is accompanied by a trusty servant
(Pedro) who passes for her brother during the voyage. The shipwreck is
fortunate, for, though it separates her from Pedro, it saves her from the
violent attentions of the shipmaster. She is washed ashore on a chest that
contains good store of coin and sundry suits of the captain's clothes. Under
the name of her brother Silvio (Shakespeare's Sebastian) she takes service
with Apolonius, who of course does not recognize her. He, in the meantime, has succumbed to the charms of an obdurate young widow, Julina
(Shakespeare's Olivia), and he employs Silla as his messenger with letters
and gifts. Julina falls in love with her while she is pleading her master's
cause and interrupts: 'Silvio, it is enough that you have said for your mais-
ter; from henceforthe, either speake for your self, or saie nothyng at al.'
Shakespeare's Olivia is less blunt, but equally frank (iii, 1, 117–121):

> 'O, by your leave, I pray you!
> I bade you never speak again of him;
> But, would you undertake another suit,
> I had rather hear you to solicit that
> Than music from the spheres.'

In the interval, Silvio has arrived at Constantinople, after wandering
through many cities in search of his sister, who he supposes has eloped with
Pedro. Julina falls in love with him as he is walking about the city, mistakes him for Silla, whom he resembles closely, and reproves him in gentle
terms for his coldness. He apologizes and they are secretly betrothed; but
he soon decamps, to continue his quest, leaving Julina with child.

Apolonius calls upon Julina for a final answer. She replies that she is
already betrothed. Somewhat later he learns from the gossip of servants
that she has received Silvio (Silla) at her house. He infers that it is his own
man who has 'thrust his nose so farre out of joynte' and shuts Silla up in a
dungeon. She tries every means, except that of revealing her sex, to induce
him to suspend judgment, but to no purpose.

Julina visits Apolonius and begs him to show mercy to her betrothed husband. He draws his rapier and swears that he will kill Silla if she does not consent to marry Julina (cf. v, 1, 128 ff.). Silla takes Julina aside, confesses that she is a woman, and explains how she had come to Constantinople because of her love for Apolonius. Julina repeats the story to Apolonius and goes home in despair.

Apolonius, enraptured, transfers his affections to Silla on the spot, and they are married. The romantic tale of Silla's adventurous love quest spreads throughout Greece and reaches the ears of the wandering Silvio. He hastens back to Constantinople and is joyfully received by his sister and her husband. Apolonius tells him, as a matter of curious interest, how Silla had been claimed by Julina as her betrothed husband. Silvio explains the circumstances and Apolonius escorts him to Julina's house. She recognizes him and they are married. Both couples live happily forever after.

Riche's tale is based on the thirty-sixth story in Part II of Bandello's *Novelle*, which he may have known either directly or through the translation in Belleforest's *Histoires Tragiques*. Bandello seems to have taken his story from *Gl' Ingannati*, a comedy written about 1531 by some member of the Sienese academy of the Intronati, perhaps Alessandro Piccolomini. This is doubtless the play which Manningham miscalls *Inganni*. A Latin version, *Lælia*, was acted at Queen's College, Cambridge, in 1595.

In adapting Bandello's *novella* Riche has made significant changes.

There is no shipwreck in Bandello. The twins have been separated in infancy at the sack of Rome. The boy (Paolo) was captured by a German who took him to Naples and treated him as his son and, at his death, left him all his property. The girl (Nicuola) fell into the hands of two Spaniards. They treated her well and she was recovered by her father (Ambrogio), who bought her for five hundred ducats. He could get no trace of Paolo. The rest of the story takes place at Esi, Ambrogio's native town. Nicuola puts on man's attire, takes the name Romulo, and acts as page and messenger for Lattantio, her own lover, who has transferred his affections to Catella, the daughter of one Gerardo, an elderly citizen of Esi and himself a suitor for Nicuola's hand. Catella falls in love with the disguised messenger. Paolo comes to Esi; she mistakes him for Romulo, and they are betrothed. Meantime Nicuola has revealed her identity to Lattantio and he has repented of his fickleness. They also pledge their troth. The *finale* is at Ambrogio's house. He is overjoyed at the sudden appearance of his long-lost son and accepts Lattantio as son-in-law. Gerardo consents to the match between Catella and Paolo. All are happy except Gerardo, who has lost his chance of winning Nicuola.

The significance of a study of sources lies in the opportunity it gives to see Shakespeare at work. The most casual comparison of Riche's novel with TWELFTH NIGHT reveals what Shakespeare has done in the mere matter of plot. Characterization one does not expect of an Elizabethan writer of short stories. That Riche's men and women are puppets is no discredit to Riche; for that is all they need be: he is telling a tale: he is not bringing men and women before us (on the stage) in their habits as they lived. Viola and Olivia and Duke Orsino have their prototypes in Riche, but are Shakespeare's own delightful creations. Sebastian is lightly sketched, but is quite worthy to be Viola's brother. No plausible suggestion has ever been made as to a source for the underplot; nor is it profitable to identify its characters with other chracters in Shakespeare. Sir Toby is not Falstaff, nor is Sir Andrew our good friend Slender. Somehow, one thinks that poor Yorick must have resembled Feste— the merriest of all Shakespeare's fools.

TWELFTH NIGHT;
OR, WHAT YOU WILL

[Dramatis Personæ.

Orsino, Duke of Illyria.
Sebastian, a young gentleman, brother of *Viola.*
Antonio, a sea captain, friend to *Sebastian.*
A Sea Captain, friend to *Viola.*
Valentine,
Curio, } gentlemen attending on the *Duke.*
Sir Toby Belch, uncle to *Olivia*
Sir Andrew Aguecheek.
Malvolio, steward to *Olivia.*
Fabian,
Feste, a Clown, } servants to *Olivia.*

Olivia, a countess.
Viola, sister to *Sebastian.*
Maria, Olivia's woman.

Lords, a Priest, Sailors, Officers, Musicians, and Attendants.

SCENE.—*A city in Illyria, and the seacoast near by.*]

2

TWELFTH NIGHT;
OR, WHAT YOU WILL

Act I. Scene I. [*The* Duke's *Palace.*]

Enter *Orsino* (*Duke of Illyria*), *Curio,* and other *Lords* ; [with
Musicians].

Duke. If music be the food of love, play on,   Sets Musical
Give me excess of it, that, surfeiting,   Tone
The appetite may sicken, and so die.
That strain again! It had a dying fall;
O, it came o'er my ear like the sweet sound   5
That breathes upon a bank of violets,
Stealing and giving odour! Enough, no more!
'Tis not so sweet now as it was before.
O spirit of love, how quick and fresh art thou!
That, notwithstanding thy capacity   10
Receiveth as the sea, naught enters there,
Of what validity and pitch soe'er,
But falls into abatement and low price
Even in a minute! So full of shapes is fancy
That it alone is high fantastical.   15
Cur. Will you go hunt, my lord?
Duke.   What, Curio?
Cur. The hart.
Duke. Why, so I do, the noblest that I have.
O, when mine eyes did see Olivia first,
Methought she purg'd the air of pestilence!   20
That instant was I turn'd into a hart,
And my desires, like fell and cruel hounds,
E'er since pursue me.

3

Enter *Valentine*.

How now? What news from her?

Val. So please my lord, I might not be admitted.
But from her handmaid do return this answer: 25
The element itself, till seven years' heat,
Shall not behold her face at ample view;
But like a cloistress she will veiled walk,
And water once a day her chamber round
With eye-offending brine: all this to season   30
A brother's dead love, which she would keep fresh
And lasting in her sad remembrance.

Duke. O, she that hath a heart of that fine frame
To pay this debt of love but to a brother,
How will she love when the rich golden shaft   35
Hath kill'd the flock of all affections else
That live in her; when liver, brain, and heart,
These sovereign thrones, are all supplied and fill'd,
Her sweet perfections, with one self king!
Away before me to sweet beds of flow'rs!   40
Love-thoughts lie rich when canopied with bow'rs.

Exeunt.

Scene II. [*The seacoast.*]

Enter *Viola*, a *Captain*, and *Sailors*.

Vio. What country, friends, is this?
Capt. This is Illyria, lady.
Vio. And what should I do in Illyria?
My brother he is in Elysium.
Perchance he is not drown'd. What think you, sailors?   5
Capt. It is perchance that you yourself were sav'd.

Vio. O my poor brother! and so perchance may he be.

Capt. True, madam; and, to comfort you with chance,
Assure yourself, after our ship did split,
When you, and those poor number sav'd with you,   10
Hung on our driving boat, I saw your brother,
Most provident in peril, bind himself
(Courage and hope both teaching him the practice)
To a strong mast that liv'd upon the sea;
Where, like Arion on the dolphin's back,   15
I saw him hold acquaintance with the waves
So long as I could see.

Vio. For saying so, there's gold.
Mine own escape unfoldeth to my hope,
Whereto thy speech serves for authority,   20
The like of him. Know'st thou this country?

Capt. Ay, madam, well, for I was bred and born
Not three hours' travel from this very place.

Vio. Who governs here?

Capt. A noble duke, in nature as in name.   25

Vio. What is his name?

Capt. Orsino.

Vio. Orsino! I have heard my father name him.
He was a bachelor then.

Capt. And so is now, or was so very late;   30
For but a month ago I went from hence,
And then 'twas fresh in murmur (as you know
What great ones do, the less will prattle of)
That he did seek the love of fair Olivia.

Vio. What's she?   35

Capt. A virtuous maid, the daughter of a count
That died some twelvemonth since; then leaving her
In the protection of his son, her brother,
Who shortly also died; for whose dear love,

They say, she hath abjur'd the company   40
And sight of men.
    Vio.   O that I serv'd that lady,
And might not be delivered to the world,
Till I had made mine own occasion mellow,
What my estate is!
    Capt.   That were hard to compass,
Because she will admit no kind of suit;   45
No, not the Duke's.
    Vio. There is a fair behaviour in thee, Captain;
And though that nature with a beauteous wall
Doth oft close in pollution, yet of thee
I will believe thou hast a mind that suits   50
With this thy fair and outward character.
I prithee (and I'll pay thee bounteously)
Conceal me what I am, and be my aid
For such disguise as haply shall become
The form of my intent. I'll serve this duke,   55
Thou shalt present me as an eunuch to him;
It may be worth thy pains. For I can sing,
And speak to him in many sorts of music
That will allow me very worth his service.
What else may hap, to time I will commit;   60
Only shape thou thy silence to my wit.
    Capt. Be you his eunuch, and your mute I'll be.
When my tongue blabs, then let mine eyes not see.
    Vio. I thank thee. Lead me on.
                               Exeunt.

Scene III. [Olivia's *house*.]

Enter Sir Toby and Maria.

To. What a plague means my niece to take the death of her brother thus? I am sure care's an enemy to life.

Mar. By my troth, Sir Toby, you must come in earlier o' nights. Your cousin, my lady, takes great exceptions to your ill hours.   6

To. Why, let her except before excepted!

Mar. Ay, but you must confine yourself within the modest limits of order.   9

To. Confine? I'll confine myself no finer than I am. These clothes are good enough to drink in, and so be these boots too. An they be not, let them hang themselves in their own straps.

Mar. That quaffing and drinking will undo you. I heard my lady talk of it yesterday; and of a foolish knight that you brought in one night here to be her wooer.   17

To. Who? Sir Andrew Aguecheek?

Mar. Ay, he.

To. He's as tall a man as any 's in Illyria.   20

Mar. What's that to th' purpose?

To. Why, he has three thousand ducats a year.

Mar. Ay, but he'll have but a year in all these ducats. He's a very fool and a prodigal.

To. Fie that you'll say so! He plays o' th' viol-de-gamboys, and speaks three or four languages word for word without book, and hath all the good gifts of nature.   29

Mar. He hath, indeed, almost natural! for, besides that he's a fool, he's a great quarreller; and but that he hath the gift of a coward to allay the gust he hath in quarrelling, 'tis thought among the prudent he would quickly have the gift of a grave.

To. By this hand, they are scoundrels and substractors that say so of him. Who are they?

Mar. They that add, moreover, he's drunk nightly in your company.   39

To. With drinking healths to my niece. I'll drink to her as long as there is a passage in my throat and drink in Illyria. He's a coward and a coystrill that will not drink to my niece till his brains turn o' th' toe like a parish top. What, wench! Castiliano vulgo! for here comes Sir Andrew Agueface. 46

Enter *Sir Andrew*.

And. Sir Toby Belch! How now, Sir Toby Belch?

To. Sweet Sir Andrew!

And. Bless you, fair shrew.   50

Mar. And you too, sir.

To. Accost, Sir Andrew, accost.

And. What's that?

To. My niece's chambermaid.

And. Good Mistress Accost, I desire better acquaintance. 56

Mar. My name is Mary, sir.

And. Good Mistress Mary Accost—

To. You mistake, knight. 'Accost' is front her, board her, woo her, assail her.   60

And. By my troth, I would not undertake her in this company. Is that the meaning of 'accost'?

Mar. Fare you well, gentlemen.

To. An thou let part so, Sir Andrew, would thou mightst never draw sword again!   66

And. An you part so, mistress, I would I might never draw sword again! Fair lady, do you think you have fools in hand?

Mar. Sir, I have not you by th' hand.   70

And. Marry, but you shall have! and here's my hand.

Mar. Now, sir, thought is free. I pray you, bring your hand to th' butt'ry bar and let it drink.

And. Wherefore, sweetheart? What's your metaphor? 76

Mar. It's dry, sir.

And. Why, I think so. I am not such an ass but I can keep my hand dry. But what's your jest? 80

Mar. A dry jest, sir.

And. Are you full of them?

Mar. Ay, sir, I have them at my fingers' ends. Marry, now I let go your hand, I am barren. *Exit.*

To. O knight, thou lack'st a cup of canary! When did I see thee so put down? 86

And. Never in your life, I think, unless you see canary put me down. Methinks sometimes I have no more wit than a Christian or an ordinary man has. But I am a great eater of beef, and I believe that does harm to my wit. 91

To. No question.

And. An I thought that, I'd forswear it. I'll ride home to-morrow, Sir Toby.

To. Pourquoi, my dear knight?

And. What is 'pourquoi'? Do, or not do? I would I had bestowed that time in the tongues that I have in fencing, dancing, and bear-baiting. O, had I but followed the arts!

To. Then hadst thou had an excellent head of hair. 101

And. Why, would that have mended my hair?

To. Past question, for thou seest it will not curl by nature. 105

And. But it becomes me well enough, does't not?

To. Excellent. It hangs like flax on a distaff; and I hope to see a housewife take thee between her legs and spin it off. 110

And. Faith, I'll home to-morrow, Sir Toby. Your niece will not be seen; or if she be, it's four to one she'll none of me. The Count himself here hard by wooes her. 114

To. She'll none o' th' Count. She'll not match above her degree, neither in estate, years, nor wit; I have heard her swear't. Tut, there's life in't, man.   118

And. I'll stay a month longer. I am a fellow o' th' strangest mind i' th' world. I delight in masques and revels sometimes altogether.   121

To. Art thou good at these kickshawses, knight?

And. As any man in Illyria, whatsoever he be, under the degree of my betters; and yet I will not compare with an old man.   126

To. What is thy excellence in a galliard, knight?

And. Faith, I can cut a caper.

To. And I can cut the mutton to't.   130

And. And I think I have the back-trick simply as strong as any man in Illyria.

To. Wherefore are these things hid? Wherefore have these gifts a curtain before 'em? Are they like to take dust, like Mistress Mall's picture? Why dost thou not go to church in a galliard and come home in a coranto? My very walk should be a jig. I would not so much as make water but in a sink-a-pace. What dost thou mean? Is it a world to hide virtues in? I did think, by the excellent constitution of thy leg, it was form'd under the star of a galliard.

And. Ay, 'tis strong, and it does indifferent well in a flame-colour'd stock. Shall we set about some revels?   145

To. What shall we do else? Were we not born under Taurus?

And. Taurus? That's sides and heart.

To. No, sir; it is legs and thighs. Let me see thee caper, [*Sir Andrew dances.*] Ha, higher! Ha, ha, excellent!

                                                            Exeunt.

Scene IV. [*The* Duke's *Palace*.]

Enter Valentine, *and* Viola *in man's attire.*

Val. If the Duke continue these favours towards you,
Cesario, you are like to be much advanc'd. He hath known
you but three days, and already you are no stranger.			4

Vio. You either fear his humour or my negligence, that you
call in question the continuance of his love. Is he inconstant,
sir, in his favours?

Val. No, believe me.

Enter Duke, Curio, *and* Attendants.

Vio. I thank you. Here comes the Count.

Duke. Who saw Cesario, ho?			10

Vio. On your attendance, my lord, here.

Duke. Stand you awhile aloof.—Cesario,
Thou know'st no less but all. I have unclasp'd
To thee the book even of my secret soul.
Therefore, good youth, address thy gait unto her;			15
Be not denied access, stand at her doors,
And tell them there thy fixed foot shall grow
Till thou have audience.

Vio.				Sure, my noble lord,
If she be so abandon'd to her sorrow
As it is spoke, she never will admit me.			20

Duke. Be clamorous and leap all civil bounds
Rather than make unprofited return.

Vio. Say I do speak with her, my lord, what then?

Duke. O, then unfold the passion of my love;
Surprise her with discourse of my dear faith!			25
It shall become thee well to act my woes.

She will attend it better in thy youth
Than in a nuncio's of more grave aspect.
  Vio. I think not so, my lord.
  Duke.   Dear lad, believe it;
For they shall yet belie thy happy years   30
That say thou art a man. Diana's lip
Is not more smooth and rubious; thy small pipe
Is as the maiden's organ, shrill and sound,
And all is semblative a woman's part.
I know thy constellation is right apt   35
For this affair. Some four or five attend him—
All, if you will; for I myself am best
When least in company. Prosper well in this,
And thou shalt live as freely as thy lord
To call his fortunes thine.
  Vio.   I'll do my best   40
To woo your lady. [*Aside*] yet a barful strife!
Whoe'er I woo, myself would be his wife.
                               Exeunt.

Scene V. [Olivia's *house*.]

Enter *Maria* and *Clown*.

  Mar. Nay, either tell me where thou hast been, or I will not open my lips so wide as a bristle may enter in way of thy excuse. My lady will hang thee for thy absence.

  Clown. Let her hang me! He that is well hang'd in this world needs to fear no colours.   6

  Mar. Make that good.

  Clown. He shall see none to fear.

  Mar. A good lenten answer. I can tell thee where that saying was born, of 'I fear no colours.'   10

  Clown. Where, good Mistress Mary?

Mar. In the wars; and that may you be bold to say in your foolery.

Clown. Well, God give them wisdom that have it; and those that are fools, let them use their talents. 16

Mar. Yet you will be hang'd for being so long absent, or to be turn'd away—is not that as good as a hanging to you?

Clown. Many a good hanging prevents a bad marriage; and for turning away, let summer bear it out. 22

Mar. You are resolute then?

Clown. Not so, neither; but I am resolv'd on two points.

Mar. That if one break, the other will hold; or if both break, your gaskins fall.

Clown. Apt, in good faith; very apt. Well, go thy way! If Sir Toby would leave drinking, thou wert as witty a piece of Eve's flesh as any in Illyria. 31

Mar. Peace, you rogue; no more o' that. Here comes my lady. Make your excuse wisely, you were best. [*Exit.*]

Enter *Lady Olivia* with *Malvolio.*

Clown. Wit, an't be thy will, put me into good fooling! Those wits that think they have thee do very oft prove fools; and I that am sure I lack thee may pass for a wise man. For what says Quinapalus? 'Better a witty fool than a foolish wit.'—God bless thee, lady! 40

Oli. Take the fool away.

Clown. Do you not hear, fellows? Take away the lady.

Oli. Go to, y'are a dry fool! I'll no more of you. Besides, you grow dishonest. 46

Clown. Two faults, madonna, that drink and good counsel will amend. For give the dry fool drink, then is the fool not dry. Bid the dishonest man mend himself: if he mend, he is no longer dishonest; if he cannot, let the botcher mend him. Anything that's mended is but patch'd; virtue that transgresses is but patch'd with sin, and sin that amends is but patch'd with virtue. If that this simple syllogism will serve, so; if it will not, what remedy? As there is no true cuckold but calamity, so beauty's a flower. The lady bade take away the fool; therefore, I say again, take her away.

Oli. Sir, I bade them take away you. 60

Clown. Misprision in the highest degree! Lady, cucullus non facit monachum. That's as much to say as, I wear not motley in my brain. Good madonna, give me leave to prove you a fool.

Oli. Can you do it? 65

Clown. Dexteriously, good madonna.

Oli. Make your proof.

Clown. I must catechize you for it, madonna. Good my mouse of virtue, answer me.

Oli. Well, sir, for want of other idleness, I'll bide your proof. 71

Clown. Good madonna, why mourn'st thou?

Oli. Good fool, for my brother's death.

Clown. I think his soul is in hell, madonna.

Oli. I know his soul is in heaven, fool. 75

Clown. The more fool, madonna, to mourn for your brother's soul, being in heaven. Take away the fool, gentlemen.

Oli. What think you of this fool, Malvolio? Doth he not mend? 80

Mal. Yes, and shall do till the pangs of death shake him. Infirmity, that decays the wise, doth ever make the better fool.

Clown. God send you, sir, a speedy infirmity, for the better increasing your folly! Sir Toby will be sworn that I am no fox; but he will not pass his word for twopence that you are no fool.

Oli. How say you to that, Malvolio? 88

Mal. I marvel your ladyship takes delight in such a barren rascal. I saw him put down the other day with an ordinary fool that has no more brain than a stone. Look you now, he's out of his guard already. Unless you laugh and minister occasion to him, he is gagg'd. I protest I take these wise men that crow so at these set kind of fools no better than the fools' zanies.

Oli. O, you are sick of self-love, Malvolio, and taste with a distemper'd appetite. To be generous, guiltless, and of free disposition, is to take those things for birdbolts that you deem cannon bullets. There is no slander in an allow'd fool, though he do nothing but rail; nor no railing in a known discreet man, though he do nothing but reprove.

Clown. Now Mercury indue thee with leasing, for thou speak'st well of fools! 106

Enter *Maria.*

Mar. Madam, there is at the gate a young gentleman much desires to speak with you.

Oli. From the Count Orsino, is it?

Mar. I know not, madam. 'Tis a fair young man, and well attended. 111

Oli. Who of my people hold him in delay?

Mar. Sir Toby, madam, your kinsman.

Oli. Fetch him off, I pray you. He speaks nothing but madman. Fie on him! [*Exit Maria.*] Go you, Malvolio. If it be a suit from the Count, I am sick, or not at home. What you will, to dismiss it. (*Exit Malvolio.*) Now you see, sir, how your fooling grows old, and people dislike it. 119

Clown. Thou hast spoke for us, madonna, as if thy eldest son should be a fool; whose skull Jove cram with brains!

Enter *Sir Toby*.

for—here he comes—one of thy kin has a most weak pia
mater.

Oli. By mine honour, half drunk! What is he at the gate,
cousin?   125

Clown. Good Sir Toby!

To. A gentleman.

Oli. A gentleman? What gentleman?

To. 'Tis a gentleman here. A plague o' these pickle-herring!
How now, sot?   130

Oli. Cousin, cousin, how have you come so early by this
lethargy?

To. Lechery? I defy lechery. There's one at the gate.

Oli. Ay, marry, what is he?   135

To. Let him be the devil an he will, I care not! Give me
faith, say I. Well, it's all one.   *Exit.*

Oli. What's a drunken man like, fool?

Clown. Like a drown'd man, a fool, and a madman. One
draught above heat makes him a fool, the second mads him,
and a third drowns him.   141

Oli. Go thou and seek the crowner, and let him sit o' my
coz; for he's in the third degree of drink—he's drown'd. Go
look after him.

Clown. He is but mad yet, madonna, and the fool shall look
to the madman.   [*Exit.*]

Enter *Malvolio*.

Mal. Madam, yond young fellow swears he will speak with
you. I told him you were sick: he takes on him to understand
so much, and therefore comes to speak with you. I told him
you were asleep: he seems to have a foreknowledge of that too,
and therefore comes to speak with you. What is to be said to
him, lady? He's fortified against any denial.

Oli. Tell him he shall not speak with me.   155

Mal. Has been told so; and he says he'll stand at your door like a sheriff's post, and be the supporter to a bench, but he'll speak with you.

Oli. What kind o' man is he?

Mal. Why, of mankind.   160

Oli. What manner of man?

Mal. Of very ill manner. He'll speak with you, will you or no.

Oli. Of what personage and years is he?   164

Mal. Not yet old enough for a man nor young enough for a boy; as a squash is before 'tis a peascod, or a codling when 'tis almost an apple. 'Tis with him in standing water, between boy and man. He is very well-favour'd and he speaks very shrewishly. One would think his mother's milk were scarce out of him.

Oli. Let him approach. Call in my gentlewoman.   173

Mal. Gentlewoman, my lady calls.   *Exit.*

Enter *Maria.*

Oli. Give me my veil; come, throw it o'er my face.   175
We'll once more hear Orsino's embassy.

Enter *Viola.*

Vio. The honourable lady of the house, which is she?

Oli. Speak to me; I shall answer for her. Your will?   180

Vio. Most radiant, exquisite, and unmatchable beauty—I pray you tell me if this be the lady of the house, for I never saw her. I would be loath to cast away my speech; for, besides that it is excellently well penn'd, I have taken great pains to con it. Good beauties, let me sustain no scorn. I am very comptible, even to the least sinister usage.

Oli. Whence came you, sir?   189

Vio. I can say little more than I have studied, and that question's out of my part. Good gentle one, give me modest assurance if you be the lady of the house, that I may proceed in my speech.

Oli. Are you a comedian?   194

Vio. No, my profound heart; and yet (by the very fangs of malice I swear) I am not that I play. Are you the lady of the house?

Oli. If I do not usurp myself, I am.   198

Vio. Most certain, if you are she, you do usurp yourself; for what is yours to bestow is not yours to reserve. But this is from my commission. I will on with my speech in your praise and then show you the heart of my message.

Oli. Come to what is important in't. I forgive you the praise.   205

Vio. Alas, I took great pains to study it, and 'tis poetical.

Oli. It is the more like to be feigned; I pray you keep it in. I heard you were saucy at my gates; and allow'd your approach rather to wonder at you than to hear you. If you be not mad, be gone; if you have reason, be brief. 'Tis not that time of moon with me to make one in so skipping a dialogue.

Mar. Will you hoist sail, sir? Here lies your way.   216

Vio. No, good swabber; I am to hull here a little longer. Some mollification for your giant, sweet lady!

Oli. Tell me your mind.

Vio. I am a messenger.   220

Oli. Sure you have some hideous matter to deliver, when the courtesy of it is so fearful. Speak your office.

Vio. It alone concerns your ear. I bring no overture of war, no taxation of homage. I hold the olive in my hand. My words are as full of peace as matter.   227

Oli. Yet you began rudely. What are you? What would you?

Vio. The rudeness that hath appear'd in me have I learn'd from my entertainment. What I am, and what I would, are as secret as maidenhead: to your ears, divinity; to any other's, profanation.   234

Oli. Give us the place alone; we will hear this divinity. [*Exit Maria.*] Now, sir, what is your text?

Vio. Most sweet lady—

Oli. A comfortable doctrine, and much may be said of it. Where lies your text?

Vio. In Orsino's bosom.

Oli. In his bosom? In what chapter of his bosom?

Vio. To answer by the method, in the first of his heart.   245

Oli. O, I have read it! it is heresy. Have you no more to say?

Vio. Good madam, let me see your face.

Oli. Have you any commission from your lord to negotiate with my face? You are now out of your text. But we will draw the curtain and show you the picture. [*Unveils.*] Look you, sir, such a one I was this present. Is't not well done?

Vio. Excellently done, if God did all.

Oli. 'Tis in grain, sir; 'twill endure wind and weather.   256

Vio. 'Tis beauty truly blent, whose red and white
Nature's own sweet and cunning hand laid on.
Lady, you are the cruell'st she alive
If you will lead these graces to the grave,   260
And leave the world no copy.

Oli. O, sir, I will not be so hard-hearted. I will give out divers schedules of my beauty. It shall be inventoried, and every particle and utensil labell'd to my will:—as, item, two lips, indifferent red; item, two grey eyes, with lids to them; item, one neck, one chin, and so forth. Were you sent hither to praise me?

Vio. I see you what you are—you are too proud;
But if you were the devil, you are fair.   270

My lord and master loves you. O, such love
Could be but recompens'd though you were crown'd
The nonpareil of beauty!

 Oli.   How does he love me?

 Vio. With adorations, with fertile tears,
With groans that thunder love, with sighs of fire. 275

 Oli. Your lord does know my mind; I cannot love him.
Yet I suppose him virtuous, know him noble,
Of great estate, of fresh and stainless youth;
In voices well divulg'd, free, learn'd, and valiant,
And in dimension and the shape of nature 280
A gracious person. But yet I cannot love him.
He might have took his answer long ago.

 Vio. If I did love you in my master's flame,
With such a suff'ring, such a deadly life,
In your denial I would find no sense; 285
I would not understand it.

 Oli.   Why, what would you?

 Vio. Make me a willow cabin at your gate
And call upon my soul within the house;
Write loyal cantons of contemned love
And sing them loud even in the dead of night; 290
Halloa your name to the reverberate hills
And make the babbling gossip of the air
Cry out 'Olivia!' O, you should not rest
Between the elements of air and earth
But you should pity me! 295

 Oli. You might do much. What is your parentage?

 Vio. Above my fortunes, yet my state is well.
I am a gentleman.

 Oli.   Get you to your lord.
I cannot love him. Let him send no more,
Unless, perchance, you come to me again 300

To tell me how he takes it. Fare you well.
I thank you for your pains. Spend this for me.
   Vio. I am no fee'd post, lady; keep your purse;
My master, not myself, lacks recompense.
Love make his heart of flint that you shall love;   305
And let your fervour, like my master's, be
Plac'd in contempt! Farewell, fair cruelty.   *Exit.*
   Oli. 'What is your parentage?'
'Above my fortunes, yet my state is well.
I am a gentleman.' I'll be sworn thou art.   310
Thy tongue, thy face, thy limbs, actions, and spirit
Do give thee fivefold blazon. Not too fast! soft, soft!
Unless the master were the man. How now?
Even so quickly may one catch the plague?
Methinks I feel this youth's perfections   315
With an invisible and subtle stealth
To creep in at mine eyes. Well, let it be.
What ho, Malvolio!

            Enter Malvolio.

   Mal.   Here, madam, at your service.
   Oli. Run after that same peevish messenger,
The County's man. He left this ring behind him,   320
Would I or not. Tell him I'll none of it.
Desire him not to flatter with his lord
Nor hold him up with hopes. I am not for him.
If that the youth will come this way to-morrow,
I'll give him reasons for't. Hie thee, Malvolio.   325
   Mal. Madam, I will.   *Exit.*
   Oli. I do know not what, and fear to find
Mine eye too great a flatterer for my mind.
Fate, show thy force! Ourselves we do not owe.   329
What is decreed must be—and be this so!   *[Exit.]*

Enter *Antonio* and *Sebastian*.

Ant. Will you stay no longer? nor will you not that I go
with you?

Seb. By your patience, no. My stars shine darkly over me;
the malignancy of my fate might perhaps distemper yours.
Therefore I shall crave of you your leave, that I may bear my
evils alone. It were a bad recompense for your love to lay any
of them on you.

Ant. Let me yet know of you whither you are bound.   10

Seb. No, sooth, sir. My determinate voyage is mere extravagancy. But I perceive in you so excellent a touch of
modesty that you will not extort from me what I am willing
to keep in; therefore it charges me in manners the rather to
express myself. You must know of me then, Antonio, my name
is Sebastian, which I call'd Roderigo. My father was that
Sebastian of Messaline whom I know you have heard of. He
left behind him myself and a sister, both born in an hour. If
the heavens had been pleas'd, would we had so ended! But
you, sir, alter'd that, for some hour before you took me from
the breach of the sea was my sister drown'd.

Ant. Alas the day!   25

Seb. A lady, sir, though it was said she much resembled me,
was yet of many accounted beautiful. But though I could not
with such estimable wonder overfar believe that, yet thus far
I will boldly publish her: she bore a mind that envy could
not but call fair. She is drown'd already, sir, with salt water,
though I seem to drown her remembrance again with more.

Ant. Pardon me, sir, your bad entertainment.

Seb. O good Antonio, forgive me your trouble!   35

Ant. If you will not murther me for my love, let me be
your servant.

22

Seb. If you will not undo what you have done, that is, kill him whom you have recover'd, desire it not. Fare ye well at once. My bosom is full of kindness; and I am yet so near the manners of my mother that, upon the least occasion more, mine eyes will tell tales of me. I am bound to the Count Orsino's court. Farewell. *Exit.*

Ant. The gentleness of all the gods go with thee! 45
I have many enemies in Orsino's court,
Else would I very shortly see thee there.
But come what may, I do adore thee so
That danger shall seem sport, and I will go. *Exit.*

Scene II. [*A street.*]

Enter *Viola* and *Malvolio* at several doors.

Mal. Were not you ev'n now with the Countess Olivia?

Vio. Even now, sir. On a moderate pace I have since arriv'd but hither. 4

Mal. She returns this ring to you, sir. You might have saved me my pains, to have taken it away yourself. She adds, moreover, that you should put your lord into a desperate assurance she will none of him. And one thing more, that you be never so hardy to come again in his affairs, unless it be to report your lord's taking of this. Receive it so. 12

Vio. She took the ring of me. I'll none of it.

Mal. Come, sir, you peevishly threw it to her; and her will is, it should be so return'd. If it be worth stooping for, there it lies, in your eye; if not, be it his that finds it. *Exit.*

Vio. I left no ring with her. What means this lady? 18
Fortune forbid my outside have not charm'd her!
She made good view of me; indeed, so much 20
That, as methought, her eyes had lost her tongue,

For she did speak in starts distractedly.
She loves me sure; the cunning of her passion
Invites me in this churlish messenger.
None of my lord's ring? Why, he sent her none!   25
I am the man. If it be so—as 'tis—
Poor lady, she were better love a dream!
Disguise, I see thou art a wickedness
Wherein the pregnant enemy does much.
How easy is it for the proper false   30
In women's waxen hearts to set their forms!
Alas, our frailty is the cause, not we!
For such as we are made of, such we be.
How will this fadge? My master loves her dearly;
And I (poor monster) fond as much on him;   35
And she (mistaken) seems to dote on me.
What will become of this? As I am man,
My state is desperate for my master's love.
As I am woman (now alas the day!),
What thriftless sighs shall poor Olivia breathe!   40
O Time, thou must untangle this, not I;
It is too hard a knot for me t' untie!   [*Exit.*]

<hr>

Scene III. [Olivia's *house*.]

<hr>

Enter *Sir Toby* and *Sir Andrew.*

To. Approach, Sir Andrew. Not to be abed after midnight
is to be up betimes; and 'diluculo surgere,' thou know'st—

And. Nay, by my troth, I know not; but I know to be up
late is to be up late.   5

To. A false conclusion! I hate it as an unfill'd can. To be
up after midnight, and to go to bed then, is early; so that to
go to bed after midnight is to go to bed betimes. Does not our
life consist of the four elements?   10

And. Faith, so they say; but I think it rather consists of eating and drinking.

To. Th'art a scholar! Let us therefore eat and drink. Marian I say! a stoup of wine!

Enter *Clown*.

And. Here comes the fool, i' faith.   15

Clown. How now, my hearts? Did you never see the picture of We Three?

To. Welcome, ass. Now let's have a catch.

And. By my troth, the fool has an excellent breast. I had rather than forty shillings I had such a leg, and so sweet a breath to sing, as the fool has. In sooth, thou wast in very gracious fooling last night, when thou spok'st of Pigrogromitus, of the Vapians passing the equinoctial of Queubus. 'Twas very good, i' faith. I sent thee sixpence for thy leman. Hadst it?

Clown. I did impeticos thy gratillity; for Malvolio's nose is no whipstock. My lady has a white hand, and the Myrmidons are no bottle-ale houses.

And. Excellent! Why, this is the best fooling, when all is done. Now a song!   31

To. Come on! there is sixpence for you. Let's have a song.

And. There's a testril of me too. If one knight give a—   35

Clown. Would you have a love song, or a song of good life?

To. A love song, a love song.

And. Ay, ay! I care not for good life.

Clown sings.

> O mistress mine, where are you roaming?   40
> O, stay and hear! your true-love 's coming,
>   That can sing both high and low.
> Trip no further, pretty sweeting;
> Journeys end in lovers meeting,
>   Every wise man's son doth know.   45

And. Excellent good, i' faith!

To. Good, good!

Clown [*sings*].

> What is love? 'Tis not hereafter;
> Present mirth hath present laughter;
>   What's to come is still unsure: 50
> In delay there lies no plenty;
> Then come kiss me, sweet and twenty!
>   Youth's a stuff will not endure.

And. A mellifluous voice, as I am true knight. 55

To. A contagious breath.

And. Very sweet and contagious, i' faith.

To. To hear by the nose, it is dulcet in contagion. But shall we make the welkin dance indeed? Shall we rouse the night owl in a catch that will draw three souls out of one weaver? Shall we do that? 62

And. An you love me, let's do't! I am dog at a catch.

Clown. By'r Lady, sir, and some dogs will catch well. 65

And. Most certain. Let our catch be 'Thou knave.'

Clown. 'Hold thy peace, thou knave,' knight? I shall be constrain'd in't to call thee knave, knight. 70

And. 'Tis not the first time I have constrained one to call me knave. Begin, fool. It begins, 'Hold thy peace.'

Clown. I shall never begin if I hold my peace.

And. Good, i' faith! Come, begin. 75

Catch sung. Enter *Maria*.

Mar. What a caterwauling do you keep here! If my lady have not call'd up her steward Malvolio and bid him turn you out of doors, never trust me. 79

To. My lady's a Catayan, we are politicians, Malvolio's a Peg-a-Ramsey, and [*sings*] 'Three merry men be we.' Am

not I consanguineous? Am I not of her blood? Tilly-vally,
lady! [*sings*] 'There dwelt a man in Babylon, lady, lady!'

Clown. Beshrew me, the knight's in admirable fooling. 86

And. Ay, he does well enough if he be dispos'd, and so do
I too. He does it with a better grace, but I do it more natural.

To. [*sings*] 'O' the twelf day of December'—

Mar. For the love o' God, peace! 92

Enter *Malvolio.*

Mal. My masters, are you mad? or what are you? Have
you no wit, manners, nor honesty, but to gabble like tinkers at
this time of night? Do ye make an alehouse of my lady's
house, that ye squeak out your coziers' catches without any
mitigation or remorse of voice? Is there no respect of place,
persons, nor time in you?

To. We did keep time, sir, in our catches. Sneck up! 101

Mal. Sir Toby, I must be round with you. My lady bade
me tell you that, though she harbours you as her kinsman,
she's nothing allied to your disorders. If you can separate
yourself and your misdemeanours, you are welcome to the
house. If not, and it would please you to take leave of her,
she is very willing to bid you farewell.

To. [*sings*] 'Farewell, dear heart since I must needs be
gone.' 110

Mar. Nay, good Sir Toby!

Clown. [*sings*] 'His eyes do show his days are almost done.'

Mal. Is't even so?

To. 'But I will never die.' 115

Clown. Sir Toby, there you lie.

Mal. This is much credit to you!

To. 'Shall I bid him go?'

Clown. 'What an if you do?'

To. 'Shall I bid him go, and spare not?' 120

Clown. 'O, no, no, no, no, you dare not!'

To. Out o' tune, sir? Ye lie. Art any more than a steward? Dost thou think, because thou art virtuous, there shall be no more cakes and ale? 125

Clown. Yes, by Saint Anne! and ginger shall be hot i' th' mouth too.

To. Th'art i' th' right.—Go, sir, rub your chain with crumbs. A stoup of wine, Maria!

Mal. Mistress Mary, if you priz'd my lady's favour at anything more than contempt, you would not give means for this uncivil rule. She shall know of it, by this hand. *Exit.*

Mar. Go shake your ears! 134

And. 'Twere as good a deed as to drink when a man's ahungry, to challenge him the field, and then to break promise with him and make a fool of him. 138

To. Do't, knight. I'll write thee a challenge; or I'll deliver thy indignation to him by word of mouth.

Mar. Sweet Sir Toby, be patient for to-night. Since the youth of the Count's was to-day with my lady, she is much out of quiet. For Monsieur Malvolio, let me alone with him. If I do not gull him into a nayword, and make him a common recreation, do not think I have wit enough to lie straight in my bed. I know I can do it.

To. Possess us, possess us! Tell us something of him. 150

Mar. Marry, sir, sometimes he is a kind of Puritan.

And. O, if I thought that, I'd beat him like a dog!

To. What, for being a Puritan? Thy exquisite reason, dear knight? 156

And. I have no exquisite reason for't, but I have reason good enough.

Mar. The devil a Puritan that he is, or anything constantly but a time-pleaser; an affection'd ass, that cons state without book and utters it by great swarths; the best persuaded of

himself; so cramm'd, as he thinks, with excellencies that it is
his grounds of faith that all that look on him love him; and
on that vice in him will my revenge find notable cause to work.

To. What wilt thou do?   167

Mar. I will drop in his way some obscure epistles of love,
wherein by the colour of his beard, the shape of his leg, the
manner of his gait, the expressure of his eye, forehead, and
complexion, he shall find himself most feelingly personated.
I can write very like my lady your niece; on a forgotten matter
we can hardly make distinction of our hands.   175

To. Excellent! I smell a device.

And. I have't in my nose too.

To. He shall think by the letters that thou wilt drop that
they come from my niece, and that she's in love with him. 180

Mar. My purpose is indeed a horse of that colour.

And. And your horse now would make him an ass.

Mar. Ass, I doubt not.   185

And. O, 'twill be admirable!

Mar. Sport royal, I warrant you. I know my physic will
work with him. I will plant you two, and let the fool make
a third, where he shall find the letter. Observe his construction of it. For this night, to bed, and dream on the event.
Farewell.   *Exit.*

To. Good night, Penthesilea.

And. Before me, she's a good wench.

To. She's a beagle true-bred, and one that adores me. What
o' that?   196

And. I was ador'd once too.

To. Let's to bed, knight. Thou hadst need send for more
money.

And. If I cannot recover your niece, I 'am a foul way out.

To. Send for money, knight. If thou hast her not i' th'
end, call me Cut.

And. If I do not, never trust me, take it how you will. 205
To. Come, come; I'll go burn some sack. 'Tis too late to
go to bed now. Come, knight; come, knight.

Exeunt.

Scene IV. [*The* Duke's *Palace.*]

Enter *Duke, Viola, Curio,* and others.

Duke. Give me some music. Now good morrow, friends.
Now, good Cesario, but that piece of song,
That old and antique song we heard last night.
Methought it did relieve my passion much,
More than light airs and recollected terms   5
Of these most brisk and giddy-paced times.
Come, but one verse.

Cur. He is not here, so please your lordship, that should
sing it.

Duke. Who was it?   10

Cur. Feste the jester, my lord, a fool that the Lady Olivia's
father took much delight in. He is about the house.

Duke. Seek him out. [*Exit Curio.*] And play the tune the
while.   *Music plays.*
Come hither, boy. If ever thou shalt love,   15
In the sweet pangs of it remember me;
For such as I am all true lovers are,
Unstaid and skittish in all motions else
Save in the constant image of the creature
That is belov'd. How dost thou like this tune?   20

Vio. It gives a very echo to the seat
Where Love is thron'd.

Duke.   Thou dost speak masterly.
My life upon't, young though thou art, thine eye

Hath stay'd upon some favour that it loves.   25
Hath it not, boy?
  Vio.   A little, by your favour.
  Duke. What kind of woman is't?
  Vio.   Of your complexion.
  Duke. She is not worth thee then. What years, i' faith?
  Vio. About your years, my lord.
  Duke. Too old, by heaven! Let still the woman take   30
An elder than herself: so wears she to him,
So sways she level in her husband's heart;
For, boy, however we do praise ourselves,
Our fancies are more giddy and unfirm,
More longing, wavering, sooner lost and won,   35
Than women's are.
  Vio.   I think it well, my lord.
  Duke. Then let thy love be younger than thyself,
Or thy affection cannot hold the bent;
For women are as roses, whose fair flow'r,
Being once display'd, doth fall that very hour.   40
  Vio. And so they are; alas, that they are so!
To die, even when they to perfection grow!

Enter *Curio* and *Clown.*

  Duke. O, fellow, come, the song we had last night.
Mark it, Cesario; it is old and plain.
The spinsters and the knitters in the sun,   45
And the free maids that weave their thread with bones,
Do use to chant it. It is silly sooth,
And dallies with the innocence of love,
Like the old age.
  Clown. Are you ready, sir?   50
  Duke. Ay; prithee sing.   *Music.*

The [Clown's] Song.

Come away, come away, death,
  And in sad cypress let me be laid.
Fly away, fly away, breath;
  I am slain by a fair cruel maid.   55
My shroud of white, stuck all with yew,
  O, prepare it!
My part of death, no one so true
  Did share it.

Not a flower, not a flower sweet,   60
  On my black coffin let there be strown;
Not a friend, not a friend greet
  My poor corpse, where my bones shall be **thrown.**
A thousand thousand sighs to save,
  Lay me, O, where   65
Sad true lover never find my grave,
  To weep there!

Duke. There's for thy pains.

Clown. No pains, sir. I take pleasure in singing, sir.   70

Duke. I'll pay thy pleasure then.

Clown. Truly, sir, and pleasure will be paid one time or another.

Duke. Give me now leave to leave thee.   74

Clown. Now the melancholy god protect thee, and the tailor make thy doublet of changeable taffeta, for thy mind is a very opal! I would have men of such constancy put to sea, that their business might be everything, and their intent everywhere; for that's it that always makes a good voyage of nothing. Farewell.   81

Exit.

Duke. Let all the rest give place.

[Exeunt Curio and Attendants.]

                                    Once more, Cesario,
Get thee to yond same sovereign cruelty.
Tell her, my love, more noble than the world,
Prizes not quantity of dirty lands.   85
The parts that fortune hath bestow'd upon her,
Tell her I hold as giddily as fortune';
But 'tis that miracle and queen of gems
That nature pranks her in, attracts my soul.
   Vio. But if she cannot love you, sir—   90
   Duke. I cannot be so answer'd.
   Vio.   Sooth, but you must.
Say that some lady, as perhaps there is,
Hath for your love as great a pang of heart
As you have for Olivia. You cannot love her.
You tell her so. Must she not then be answer'd?   95
   Duke. There is no woman's sides
Can bide the beating of so strong a passion
As love doth give my heart; no woman's heart
So big to hold so much; they lack retention.
Alas, their love may be call'd appetite—   100
No motion of the liver, but the palate—
That suffers surfeit, cloyment, and revolt;
But mine is all as hungry as the sea
And can digest as much. Make no compare
Between that love a woman can bear me   105
And that I owe Olivia.
   Vio.   Ay, but I know—
   Duke. What dost thou know?
   Vio. Too well what love women to men may owe.
In faith, they are as true of heart as we.
My father had a daughter lov'd a man   110
As it might be perhaps, were I a woman,
I should your lordship.

Duke.   And what's her history?

Vio. A blank, my lord. She never told her love,
But let concealment, like a worm i' th' bud,
Feed on her damask cheek. She pin'd in thought; 115
And, with a green and yellow melancholy,
She sat like Patience on a monument,
Smiling at grief. Was not this love indeed?
We men may say more, swear more; but indeed
Our shows are more than will; for still we prove 120
Much in our vows but little in our love.

Duke. But died thy sister of her love, my boy?

Vio. I am all the daughters of my father's house,
And all the brothers too—and yet I know not.
Sir, shall I to this lady?

Duke.   Ay, that's the theme. 125
To her in haste! Give her this jewel: Say
My love can give no place, bide no denay.

Exeunt.

Scene V. [Olivia's *orchard.*]

Enter *Sir Toby, Sir Andrew,* and *Fabian.*

To. Come thy ways, Signior Fabian.

Fab. Nay, I'll come. If I lose a scruple of this sport, let me
be boil'd to death with melancholy. 4

To. Wouldst thou not be glad to have the niggardly rascally
sheep-biter come by some notable shame?

Fab. I would exult, man. You know he brought me out o'
favour with my lady about a bear-baiting here. 10

To. To anger him we'll have the bear again; and we will
fool him black and blue. Shall we not, Sir Andrew?

And. An we do not, it is pity of our lives. 14

Enter *Maria*.

To. Here comes the little villain. How now, my metal of India?

Mar. Get ye all three into the box tree. Malvolio's coming down this walk. He has been yonder i' the sun practising behaviour to his own shadow this half hour. Observe him, for the love of mockery; for I know this letter will make a contemplative idiot of him. Close, in the name of jesting! [*The others hide.*] Lie thou there [*Throws down a letter*]; for here comes the trout that must be caught with tickling. *Exit.*

Enter *Malvolio*.

Mal. 'Tis but fortune; all is fortune. Maria once told me she did affect me; and I have heard herself come thus near, that, should she fancy, it should be one of my complexion. Besides, she uses me with a more exalted respect than any one else that follows her. What should I think on't?

To. Here's an overweening rogue!   34

Fab. O, peace! Contemplation makes a rare turkey cock of him. How he jets under his advanc'd plumes!

And. 'Slight, I could so beat the rogue!

Fab. Peace, I say.

Mal. To be Count Malvolio!   40

To. Ah, rogue!

And. Pistol him, pistol him!

Fab. Peace, peace!

Mal. There is example for't. The Lady of the Strachy married the yeoman of the wardrobe.   45

And. Fie on him, Jezebel!

Fab. O, peace! Now he's deeply in. Look how imagination blows him.

Mal. Having been three months married to her, sitting in
my state—   50

To. O for a stone-bow, to hit him in the eye!

Mal. Calling my officers about me, in my branch'd velvet
gown; having come from a day-bed, where I have left Olivia
sleeping—   55

To. Fire and brimstone!

Fab. O, peace, peace!

Mal. And then to have the humour of state; and after a
demure travel of regard—telling them I know my place, as I
would they should do theirs—to ask for my kinsman Toby—

To. Bolts and shackles!   62

Fab. O, peace, peace, peace! Now, now.

Mal. Seven of my people, with an obedient start, make out
for him. I frown the while, and perchance wind up my watch,
or play with my—some rich jewel. Toby approaches; curtsies
there to me—

To. Shall this fellow live?

Fab. Though our silence be drawn from us by th' ears, yet
peace!   71

Mal. I extend my hand to him thus, quenching my familiar
smile with an austere regard of control—

To. And does not Toby take you a blow o' the lips then?

Mal. Saying, 'Cousin Toby, my fortunes having cast me on
your niece, give me this prerogative of speech.'

To. What, what?   80

Mal. 'You must amend your drunkenness.'

To. Out, scab!

Fab. Nay, patience, or we break the sinews of our plot.

Mal. 'Besides, you waste the treasure of your time with a
foolish knight'—   86

And. That's me, I warrant you.

Mal. 'One Sir Andrew'—

And. I knew 'twas I, for many do call me fool.

Mal. What employment have we here?

[*Takes up the letter.*]

Fab. Now is the woodcock near the gin.

To. O, peace! and the spirit of humours intimate reading aloud to him!   94

Mal. By my life, this is my lady's hand! These be her very C's, her U's, and her T's; and thus makes she her great P's. It is, in contempt of question, her hand.

And. Her C's, her U's, and her T's? Why that?

Mal. [*reads*] 'To the unknown belov'd, this, and my good wishes.' Her very phrases! By your leave, wax. Soft! and the impressure her Lucrece, with which she uses to seal! 'Tis my lady. To whom should this be?   105

Fab. This wins him, liver and all.

Mal. [*reads*]

>   'Jove knows I love—
>   But who?
>   Lips, do not move;
>   No man must know.'   110

'No man must know.' What follows? The numbers alter'd! 'No man must know.' If this should be thee, Malvolio?

To. Marry, hang thee, brock!

Mal. [*reads*]

>   'I may command where I adore;
>   But silence, like a Lucrece knife,   115
>   With bloodless stroke my heart doth gore.
>   M. O. A. I. doth sway my life.'

Fab. A fustian riddle!

To. Excellent wench, say I.   120

Mal. 'M. O. A. I. doth sway my life.' Nay, but first, let me see, let me see, let me see.

Fab. What dish o' poison has she dress'd him!

To. And with what wing the staniel checks at it!   125

Mal. 'I may command where I adore.' Why, she may command me: I serve her; she is my lady. Why, this is evident to any formal capacity. There is no obstruction in this. And the end—what should that alphabetical position portend? If I could make that resemble something in me! Softly! M. O. A. I.   132

To. O, ay, make up that! He is now at a cold scent.

Fab. Sowter will cry upon't for all this, though it be as rank as a fox.   136

Mal. M.—Malvolio. M.—Why, that begins my name!

Fab. Did not I say he would work it out? The cur is excellent at faults.   140

Mal. M.—But then there is no consonancy in the sequel. That suffers under probation. A should follow, but O does.

Fab. And O shall end, I hope.

To. Ay, or I'll cudgel him, and make him cry O!   146

Mal. And then I comes behind.

Fab. Ay, an you had any eye behind you, you might see more detraction at your heels than fortunes before you.   150

Mal. M, O, A, I. This simulation is not as the former; and yet, to crush this a little, it would bow to me, for every one of these letters are in my name. Soft! here follows prose.   154

[*Reads*] 'If this fall into thy hand, revolve. In my stars I am above thee; but be not afraid of greatness. Some are born great, some achieve greatness, and some have greatness thrust upon 'em. Thy Fates open their hands; let thy blood and spirit embrace them; and to inure thyself to what thou art like to be, cast thy humble slough and appear fresh. Be opposite with a kinsman, surly with servants. Let thy tongue tang arguments of state; put thyself into the trick of singularity. She thus advises thee that sighs for thee. Remember who commended thy yellow stockings and wish'd to see thee ever cross-garter'd. I say, remember. Go to, thou art made, if thou desir'st to be so. If not, let me see thee a steward still, the fellow of servants, and not worthy to touch Fortune's fingers. Farewell. She that would alter services with thee,

                              'THE FORTUNATE UNHAPPY.'

Daylight and champian discovers not more. This is open. I will be proud, I will read politic authors, I will baffle Sir Toby, I will wash off gross acquaintance, I will be point-devise, the very man. I do not now fool myself, to let imagination jade me; for every reason excites to this, that my lady loves me. She did commend my yellow stockings of late, she did praise my leg being cross-garter'd; and in this she manifests herself to my love, and with a kind of injunction drives me to these habits of her liking. I thank my stars, I am happy. I will be strange, stout, in yellow stockings, and cross-garter'd, even with the swiftness of putting on. Jove and my stars be praised! Here is yet a postscript.

'Thou canst not choose but know who I am. If thou entertain'st my love, let it appear in thy smiling. Thy smiles become thee well. Therefore in my presence still smile, dear my sweet, I prithee.'

Jove, I thank thee. I will smile; I will do everything that thou wilt have me.   *Exit.*

   Fab. I will not give my part of this sport for a pension of thousands to be paid from the Sophy.

   To. I could marry this wench for this device—

   And. So could I too.   200

   To. And ask no other dowry with her but such another jest.

                          Enter *Maria.*

   And. Nor I neither.

   Fab. Here comes my noble gull-catcher.

To. Wilt thou set thy foot o' my neck? 205

Ad. Or o' mine either?

To. Shall I play my freedom at tray-trip and become thy bondslave?

And. I' faith, or I either? 209

To. Why, thou hast put him in such a dream that, when the image of it leaves him, he must run mad.

Mar. Nay, but say true, does it work upon him?

To. Like aqua-vitæ with a midwife. 215

Mar. If you will, then, see the fruits of the sport, mark his first approach before my lady. He will come to her in yellow stockings, and 'tis a colour she abhors, and cross-garter'd, a fashion she detests; and he will smile upon her, which will now be so unsuitable to her disposition, being addicted to a melancholy as she is, that it cannot but turn him into a notable contempt. If you will see it, follow me.

To. To the gates of Tartar, thou most excellent devil of wit! 226

And. I'll make one too.

Exeunt.

Enter Viola, *and* Clown [with a tabor and pipe].

Vio. Save thee, friend, and thy music! Dost thou live by thy tabor?

Clown. No, sir, I live by the church.

Vio. Art thou a churchman? 4

Clown. No such matter, sir. I do live by the church; for I do live at my house, and my house doth stand by the church.

Vio. So thou mayst say, the king lies by a beggar, if a beggar dwell near him; or, the church stands by thy tabor, if thy tabor stand by the church. 11

Clown. You have said, sir. To see this age! A sentence is but a chev'ril glove to a good wit. How quickly the wrong side may be turn'd outward! 15

Vio. Nay, that's certain. They that dally nicely with words may quickly make them wanton.

Clown. I would therefore my sister had had no name, sir.

Vio. Why, man? 21

Clown. Why, sir her name's a word, and to dally with that word might make my sister wanton. But indeed words are very rascals since bonds disgrac'd them. 25

Vio. Thy reason, man?

Clown. Troth, sir, I can yield you none without words, and words are grown so false I am loath to prove reason with them.

Vio. I warrant thou art a merry fellow and car'st for nothing. 31

Clown. Not so, sir; I do care for something; but in my conscience, sir, I do not care for you. If that be to care for nothing, sir, I would it would make you invisible. 35

Vio. Art not thou the Lady Olivia's fool?

Clown. No, indeed, sir. The Lady Olivia has no folly. She

will keep no fool, sir, till she be married; and fools are as like husbands as pilchers are to herrings—the husband's the bigger. I am indeed not her fool, but her corrupter of words.

Vio. I saw thee late at the Count Orsino's.   42

Clown. Foolery, sir, does walk about the orb like the sun; it shines everywhere. I would be sorry, sir, but the fool should be as oft with your master as with my mistress. I think I saw your wisdom there.   47

Vio. Nay, an thou pass upon me, I'll no more with thee. Hold, there's expenses for thee.   [*Gives a piece of money.*]

Clown. Now Jove, in his next commodity of hair, send thee a beard!   51

Vio. By my troth, I'll tell thee, I am almost sick for one, though I would not have it grow on my chin. Is thy lady within?

Clown. Would not a pair of these have bred, sir?   55

Vio. Yes, being kept together and put to use.

Clown. I would play Lord Pandarus of Phrygia, sir, to bring a Cressida to this Troilus.

Vio. I understand you, sir. 'Tis well begg'd.

[*Gives another piece.*]

Clown. The matter, I hope, is not great, sir, begging but a beggar: Cressida was a beggar. My lady is within, sir. I will conster to them whence you come. Who you are and what you would are out of my welkin—I might say 'element,' but the word is over-worn.   *Exit.*

Vio. This fellow is wise enough to play the fool,   67
And to do that well craves a kind of wit.
He must observe their mood on whom he jests,
The quality of persons, and the time;   70
Not, like the haggard, check at every feather
That comes before his eye. This is a practice
As full of labour as a wise man's art;

For folly that he wisely shows, is fit;
But wise men, folly-fall'n, quite taint their wit.   75

Enter *Sir Toby* and [*Sir*] *Andrew*.

To. Save you, gentleman!

Vio. And you, sir.

And. Dieu vous garde, monsieur.

Vio. Et vous aussi; vostre serviteur.

And. I hope, sir, you are, and I am yours.   80

To. Will you encounter the house? My niece is desirous
you should enter, if your trade be to her.

Vio. I am bound to your niece, sir. I mean, she is the list
of my voyage.   86

To. Taste your legs, sir; put them to motion.

Vio. My legs do better understand me, sir, than I understand what you mean by bidding me taste my legs.   91

To. I mean, to go, sir, to enter.

Vio. I will answer you with gait and entrance. But we are
prevented.

Enter *Olivia* and *Gentlewoman*, [*Maria*].

Most excellent accomplish'd lady, the heavens rain odours on
you!   96

And. [*aside*] That youth's a rare courtier. 'Rain odours'
—well!

Vio. My matter hath no voice, lady, but to your own most
pregnant and vouchsafed ear.

And. [*aside*] 'Odours,' 'pregnant,' and 'vouchsafed'—I'll
get 'em all three all ready.

Oli. Let the garden door be shut, and leave me to my hearing. [*Exeunt Sir Toby, Sir Andrew, and Maria.*] Give me
your hand, sir.

Vio. My duty, madam, and most humble service.   106

Oli. What is your name?

Vio. Cesario is your servant's name, fair princess.

Oli. My servant, sir? 'Twas never merry world
Since lowly feigning was call'd compliment.   **110**
Y'are servant to the Count Orsino, youth.

Vio. And he is yours, and his must needs be yours.
Your servant's servant is your servant, madam.

Oli. For him, I think not on him; for his thoughts,
Would they were blanks, rather than fill'd with me!   **115**

Vio. Madam, I come to whet your gentle thoughts
On his behalf.

Oli.   O, by your leave, I pray you!
I bade you never speak again of him;
But, would you undertake another suit,
I had rather hear you to solicit that   **120**
Than music from the spheres.

Vio.   Dear lady—

Oli. Give me leave, beseech you. I did send,
After the last enchantment you did here,
A ring in chase of you. So did I abuse
Myself, my servant, and, I fear me, you.   **125**
Under your hard construction must I sit,
To force that on you in a shameful cunning
Which you knew none of yours. What might you think?
Have you not set mine honour at the stake
And baited it with all th' unmuzzled thoughts   **130**
That tyrannous heart can think? To one of your receiving
Enough is shown; a cypress, not a bosom,
Hides my heart. So, let me hear you speak.

Vio. I pity you.

Oli.   That's a degree to love.

Vio. No, not a grize; for 'tis a vulgar proof   **135**
That very oft we pity enemies.

Oli. Why then, methinks 'tis time to smile again.
O world, how apt the poor are to be proud!
If one should be a prey, how much the better
To fall before the lion than the wolf!   140

Clock strikes.

The clock upbraids me with the waste of time.
Be not afraid, good youth, I will not have you;
And yet, when wit and youth is come to harvest,
Your wife is like to reap a proper man.
There lies your way, due west.

Vio.   Then westward ho!   146
Grace and good disposition attend your ladyship!
You'll nothing, madam, to my lord by me?

Oli. Stay.
I prithee tell me what thou think'st of me.   150

Vio. That you do think you are not what you are.

Oli. If I think so, I think the same of you.

Vio. Then think you right. I am not what I am.

Oli. I would you were as I would have you be!

Vio. Would it be better, madam, than I am?   155
I wish it might; for now I am your fool.

Oli. O, what a deal of scorn looks beautiful
In the contempt and anger of his lip!
A murd'rous guilt shows not itself more soon
Than love that would seem hid: love's night is noon.   160
Cesario, by the roses of the spring,
By maidhood, honour, truth, and everything,
I love thee so that, maugre all thy pride,
Nor wit nor reason can my passion hide.
Do not extort thy reasons from this clause,   165
For that I woo, thou therefore hast no cause;
But rather reason thus with reason fetter:
Love sought is good, but given unsought is better.

Vio. By innocence I swear, and by my youth,
I have one heart, one bosom, and one truth,   170
And that no woman has; nor never none
Shall mistress be of it, save I alone.
And so adieu, good madam. Never more
Will I my master's tears to you deplore.

Oli. Yet come again; for thou perhaps mayst move   175
That heart which now abhors to like his love.

Exeunt.

Scene II. [Olivia's *house.*]

Enter *Sir Toby, Sir Andrew,* and *Fabian.*

And. No, faith, I'll not stay a jot longer.

To. Thy reason, dear venom; give thy reason.

Fab. You must needs yield your reason, Sir Andrew.   5

And. Marry, I saw your niece do more favours to the Count's servingman than ever she bestow'd upon me. I saw't i' th' orchard.

To. Did she see thee the while, old boy? Tell me that.   10

And. As plain as I see you now.

Fab. This was a great argument of love in her toward you.

And. 'Slight! will you make an ass o' me?

Fab. I will prove it legitimate, sir, upon the oaths of judgment and reason.   16

To. And they have been grand-jurymen since before Noah was a sailor.

Fab. She did show favour to the youth in your sight only to exasperate you, to awake your dormouse valour, to put fire in your heart and brimstone in your liver. You should then have accosted her; and with some excellent jests, fire-new from the mint, you should have bang'd the youth into dumbness. This was look'd for at your hand, and this was balk'd. The double gilt of this opportunity you let time wash off, and you are now sail'd into the North of my lady's opinion, where you will hang like an icicle on a Dutchman's beard unless you do redeem it by some laudable attempt either of valour or policy. 31

And. An't be any way, it must be with valour; for policy I hate. I had as lief be a Brownist as a politician. 34

To. Why then, build me thy fortunes upon the basis of valour. Challenge me the Count's youth to fight with him; hurt him in eleven places. My niece shall take note of it; and assure thyself there is no love-broker in the world can more prevail in man's commendation with woman than report of valour. 41

Fab. There is no way but this, Sir Andrew.

And. Will either of you bear me a challenge to him? 44

To. Go, write it in a martial hand. Be curst and brief; it is no matter how witty, so it be eloquent and full of invention. Taunt him with the license of ink. If thou thou'st him some thrice, it shall not be amiss; and as many lies as will lie in thy sheet of paper, although the sheet were big enough for the bed of Ware in England, set 'em down. Go, about it! Let there be gall enough in thy ink, though thou write with a goose-pen, no matter. About it!

And. Where shall I find you? 55

To. We'll call thee at the cubiculo. Go.

Exit Sir Andrew.

Fab. This is a dear manikin to you, Sir Toby.

To. I have been dear to him, lad—some two thousand strong, or so.

Fab. We shall have a rare letter from him—but you'll not deliver 't? 61

To. Never trust me then; and by all means stir on the youth

to an answer. I think oxen and wainropes cannot hale them together. For Andrew, if he were open'd, and you find so much
blood in his liver as will clog the foot of a flea, I'll eat the rest
of th' anatomy.   67

Fab. And his opposite, the youth, bears in his visage no
great presage of cruelty.

Enter *Maria*.

To. Look where the youngest wren of nine comes.   71

Mar. If you desire the spleen, and will laugh yourselves into
stitches, follow me. Yond gull Malvolio is turned heathen, a
very renegado; for there is no Christian that means to be saved
by believing rightly can ever believe such impossible passages
of grossness. He's in yellow stockings!

To. And cross-garter'd?   79

Mar. Most villanously; like a pedant that keeps a school
i' th' church. I have dogg'd him like his murtherer. He does
obey every point of the letter that I dropp'd to betray him. He
does smile his face into more lines than is in the new map
with the augmentation of the Indies. You have not seen such
a thing as 'tis. I can hardly forbear hurling things at him. I
know my lady will strike him. If she do, he'll smile, and take't
for a great favour.

To. Come bring us, bring us where he is!   90

Exeunt omnes.

Scene III. [*A street.*]

Enter *Sebastian* and *Antonio*.

Seb. I would not by my will have troubled you;
But since you make your pleasure of your pains,
I will no further chide you.

Ant. I could not stay behind you. My desire,
More sharp than filed steel, did spur me forth; 5
And not all love to see you (though so much
As might have drawn one to a longer voyage)
But jealousy what might befall your travel,
Being skilless in these parts; which to a stranger,
Unguided and unfriended, often prove 10
Rough and unhospitable. My willing love,
The rather by these arguments of fear,
Set forth in your pursuit.

    Seb. My kind Antonio,
I can no other answer make but thanks,
And thanks, and ever thanks; and oft good turns 15
Are shuffled off with such uncurrent pay.
But, were my worth as is my conscience firm,
You should find better dealing. What's to do?
Shall we go see the relics of this town?

    Ant. To-morrow, sir; best first go see your lodging. 20

    Seb. I am not weary, and 'tis long to night.
I pray you let us satisfy our eyes
With the memorials and the things of fame
That do renown this city.

    Ant. Would you'ld pardon me.
I do not without danger walk these streets. 25
Once in a sea-fight 'gainst the Count his galleys
I did some service; of such note indeed
That, were I ta'en here, it would scarce be answer'd.

    Seb. Belike you slew great number of his people?

    Ant. Th' offence is not of such a bloody nature, 30
Albeit the quality of the time and quarrel
Might well have given us bloody argument.
It might have since been answer'd in repaying
What we took from them, which for traffic's sake

Most of our city did. Only myself stood out;   35
For which, if I be lapsed in this place,
I shall pay dear.

   Seb.   Do not then walk too open.

   Ant. It doth not fit me. Hold, sir, here's my purse.
In the south suburbs at the Elephant
Is best to lodge. I will bespeak our diet,   40
Whiles you beguile the time and feed your knowledge
With viewing of the town. There shall you have me.

   Seb. Why I your purse?

   Ant. Haply your eye shall light upon some toy
You have desire to purchase; and your store   45
I think is not for idle markets, sir.

   Seb. I'll be your purse-bearer, and leave you for
An hour.

   Ant.   To th' Elephant.

   Seb.   I do remember.

                                    Exeunt.

Scene IV. [Olivia's *orchard*.]

Enter *Olivia* and *Maria*.

   Oli. I have sent after him; he says he'll come.
How shall I feast him? what bestow of him?
For youth is bought more oft than begg'd or borrow'd.
I speak too loud.
Where is Malvolio? He is sad and civil,   5
And suits well for a servant with my fortunes.
Where is Malvolio?

   Mar. He's coming, madam; but in very strange manner.
He is sure possess'd, madam.

   Oli. Why, what's the matter? Does he rave?   10

Mar. No, madam, he does nothing but smile. Your ladyship were best to have some guard about you if he come, for sure the man is tainted in 's wits.

Oli. Go call him hither. [*Exit Maria.*] I am as mad as he, If sad and merry madness equal be.   16

Enter [*Maria,* with] *Malvolio.*

How now, Malvolio?

Mal. Sweet lady, ho, ho!

Oli. Smil'st thou?

I sent for thee upon a sad occasion.   20

Mal. Sad, lady? I could be sad. This does make some ob-struction in the blood, this cross-gartering; but what of that? If it please the eye of one, it is with me as the very true sonnet is, 'Please one, and please all.'   25

Oli. Why, how dost thou, man? What is the matter with thee?

Mal. Not black in my mind, though yellow in my legs. It did come to his hands, and commands shall be executed. I think we do know the sweet Roman hand.   31

Oli. Wilt thou go to bed, Malvolio?

Mal. To bed? Ay, sweetheart; and I'll come to thee.

Oli. God comfort thee! Why dost thou smile so, and kiss thy hand so oft?   36

Mar. How do you, Malvolio?

Mal. At your request? Yes, nightingales answer daws!

Mar. Why appear you with this ridiculous boldness before my lady?   41

Mal. 'Be not afraid of greatness.' 'Twas well writ.

Oli. What mean'st thou by that, Malvolio?

Mal. 'Some are born great'—   45

Oli. Ha?

Mal. 'Some achieve greatness'—

Oli. What say'st thou?

Mal. 'And some have greatness thrust upon them.' 50

Oli. Heaven restore thee!

Mal. 'Remember who commended thy yellow stockings'—

Oli. My yellow stockings?

Mal. 'And wish'd to see thee cross-garter'd.' 55

Oli. Cross-garter'd?

Mal. 'Go to, thou art made, if thou desir'st to be so'—

Oli. Am I made?

Mal. 'If not, let me see thee a servant still.' 60

Oli. Why, this is very midsummer madness.

Enter *Servant*.

Ser. Madam, the young gentleman of the Count Orsino's is return'd. I could hardly entreat him back. He attends your ladyship's pleasure. 65

Oli. I'll come to him. [*Exit Servant.*] Good Maria, let this fellow be look'd to. Where's my cousin Toby? Let some of my people have a special care of him. I would not have him miscarry for the half of my dowry. 70

Exit [*Olivia; then Maria*].

Mal. O ho! do you come near me now? No worse man than Sir Toby to look to me! This concurs directly with the letter. She sends him on purpose, that I may appear stubborn to him; for she incites me to that in the letter. 'Cast thy humble slough,' says she; 'be opposite with a kinsman, surly with servants; let thy tongue tang with arguments of state; put thyself into the trick of singularity';—and consequently sets down the manner how: as, a sad face, a reverend carriage, a slow tongue, in the habit of some sir of note, and so forth. I have lim'd her; but it is Jove's doing, and Jove make me thankful! And when she went away now, 'Let this fellow be look'd to.' 'Fellow!' not 'Malvolio,' nor after my degree, but 'fellow.' Why, every-

thing adheres together, that no dram of a scruple, no scruple
of a scruple, no obstacle, no incredulous or unsafe circumstance
—What can be said? Nothing that can be can come between
me and the full prospect of my hopes. Well, Jove, not I, is the
doer of this, and he is to be thanked.   92

Enter [*Sir*] *Toby*, *Fabian*, and *Maria*.

To. Which way is he, in the name of sanctity? If all the
devils of hell be drawn in little, and Legion himself possess'd
him, yet I'll speak to him.   96

Fab. Here he is, here he is! How is't with you, sir?

To. How is't with you, man?

Mal. Go off; I discard you. Let me enjoy my private. Go
off.   100

Mar. Lo, how hollow the fiend speaks within him! Did not
I tell you? Sir Toby, my lady prays you to have a care of him.

Mal. Aha! does she so?   104

To. Go to, go to; peace, peace! We must deal gently with
him. Let me alone. How do you, Malvolio? How is't with
you? What, man! defy the devil! Consider, he's an enemy
to mankind.

Mal. Do you know what you say?   110

Mar. La you, an you speak ill of the devil, how he takes it
at heart! Pray God he be not bewitch'd!

Fab. Carry his water to th' wise woman.   114

Mar. Marry, and it shall be done to-morrow morning if I
live. My lady would not lose him for more than I'll say.

Mal. How now, mistress?

Mar. O Lord!   119

To. Prithee hold thy peace. This is not the way. Do you
not see you move him? Let me alone with him.

Fab. No way but gentleness; gently, gently. The fiend is
rough and will not be roughly us'd.

To. Why, how now, my bawcock? How dost thou, chuck?

Mal. Sir!   127

To. Ay, biddy, come with me. What, man! 'tis not for gravity to play at cherry-pit with Satan. Hang him, foul collier!   130

Mar. Get him to say his prayers. Good Sir Toby, get him to pray.

Mal. My prayers, minx?

Mar. No, I warrant you, he will not hear of godliness. 135

Mal. Go hang yourselves all! You are idle shallow things; I am not of your element. You shall know more hereafter.

Exit.

To. Is't possible?

Fab. If this were play'd upon a stage now, I could condemn it as an improbable fiction.   141

To. His very genius hath taken the infection of the device, man.

Mar. Nay, pursue him now, lest the device take air and taint.   145

Fab. Why, we shall make him mad indeed.

Mar. The house will be the quieter.

To. Come, we'll have him in a dark room and bound. My niece is already in the belief that he's mad. We may carry it thus, for our pleasure and his penance, till our very pastime, tired out of breath, prompt us to have mercy on him; at which time we will bring the device to the bar and crown thee for a finder of madmen. But see, but see!   155

Enter *Sir Andrew.*

Fab. More matter for a May morning.

And. Here's the challenge; read it. I warrant there's vinegar and pepper in't.

Fab. Is't so saucy?

And. Ay, is't, I warrant him. Do but read.   160

To. Give me. [*Reads*] 'Youth, whatsoever thou art, thou art but a scurvy fellow.'

Fab. Good, and valiant.

To. [*reads*] 'Wonder not nor admire not in thy mind why I do call thee so, for I will show thee no reason for't.'

Fab. A good note! That keeps you from the blow of the law.   169

To. [*reads*] 'Thou com'st to the Lady Olivia, and in my sight she uses thee kindly. But thou liest in thy throat; that is not the matter I challenge thee for.'

Fab. Very brief, and to exceeding good sense—less.   175

To. [*reads*] 'I will waylay thee going home; where if it be thy chance to kill me'—

Fab. Good.

To. [*reads*] 'Thou kill'st me like a rogue and a villain.'   180

Fab. Still you keep o' th' windy side of the law. Good.

To. [*reads*] 'Fare thee well, and God have mercy upon one of our souls! He may have mercy upon mine, but my hope is better ; and so look to thyself. Thy friend, as thou usest him, and thy sworn enemy,

'ANDREW AGUECHEEK.'

If this letter move him not, his legs cannot. I'll give't him.

Mar. You may have very fit occasion for't. He is now in some commerce with my lady and will by-and-by depart.

To. Go, Sir Andrew! Scout me for him at the corner of the orchard like a bum-baily. So soon as ever thou seest him, draw; and as thou draw'st, swear horrible; for it comes to pass oft that a terrible oath, with a swaggering accent sharply twang'd off, gives manhood more approbation than ever proof itself would have earn'd him. Away!   200

And. Nay, let me alone for swearing.   *Exit.*

To. Now will not I deliver his letter; for the behaviour of the young gentleman gives him out to be of good capacity and breeding; his employment between his lord and my niece confirms no less. Therefore this letter, being so excellently ignorant, will breed no terror in the youth. He will find it comes from a clodpoll. But, sir, I will deliver his challenge by word of mouth, set upon Aguecheek a notable report of valour, and drive the gentleman (as I know his youth will aptly receive it) into a most hideous opinion of his rage, skill, fury, and impetuosity. This will so fright them both that they will kill one another by the look, like cockatrices. 215

Enter *Olivia* and *Viola*.

Fab. Here he comes with your niece. Give them way till he take leave, and presently after him.

To. I will meditate the while upon some horrid message for a challenge. 220

[*Exeunt Sir Toby, Fabian, and Maria.*]

Oli. I have said too much unto a heart of stone
And laid mine honour too unchary out.
There's something in me that reproves my fault;
But such a headstrong potent fault it is
That it but mocks reproof. 225

Vio. With the same haviour that your passion bears
Goes on my master's grief.

Oli. Here, wear this jewel for me; 'tis my picture.
Refuse it not; it hath no tongue to vex you.
And I beseech you come again to-morrow. 230
What shall you ask of me that I'll deny,
That honour, sav'd, may upon asking give?

Vio. Nothing but this—your true love for my master.

Oli. How with mine honour may I give him that
Which I have given to you?

Vio.   I will acquit you. 235

Oli. Well, come again to-morrow. Fare thee well.
A fiend like thee might bear my soul to hell. [*Exit.*]

Enter [*Sir*] *Toby* and *Fabian.*

To. Gentleman, God save thee!

Vio. And you, sir. 239

To. That defence thou hast, betake thee to't. Of what nature the wrongs are thou hast done him, I know not; but thy intercepter, full of despite, bloody as the hunter, attends thee at the orchard end. Dismount thy tuck, be yare in thy preparation; for thy assailant is quick, skilful, and deadly. 246

Vio. You mistake, sir. I am sure no man hath any quarrel to me. My remembrance is very free and clear from any image of offence done to any man. 250

To. You'll find it otherwise, I assure you. Therefore, if you hold your life at any price, betake you to your guard; for your opposite hath in him what youth, strength, skill, and wrath can furnish man withal. 255

Vio. I pray you, sir, what is he?

To. He is knight, dubb'd with unhatch'd rapier and on carpet consideration; but he is a devil in private brawl. Souls and bodies hath he divorc'd three; and his incensement at this moment is so implacable that satisfaction can be none but by pangs of death and sepulchre. 'Hob, nob' is his word; 'give't or take't.' 262

Vio. I will return again into the house and desire some conduct of the lady. I am no fighter. I have heard of some kind of men that put quarrels purposely on others to taste their valour. Belike this is a man of that quirk. 266

To. Sir, no. His indignation derives itself out of a very competent injury; therefore get you on and give him his desire. Back you shall not to the house, unless you undertake that with me which with as much safety you might answer

him. Therefore on! or strip your sword stark naked; for meddle you must, that's certain, or forswear to wear iron about you.

Vio. This is as uncivil as strange. I beseech you do me this
courteous office, as to know of the knight what my offence to
him is. It is something of my negligence, nothing of my purpose.   280

To. I will do so. Signior Fabian, stay you by this gentleman till my return.   *Exit.*

Vio. Pray you, sir, do you know of this matter?   284

Fab. I know the knight is incens'd against you, even to a
mortal arbitrement; but nothing of the circumstance more.

Vio. I beseech you, what manner of man is he?   289

Fab. Nothing of that wonderful promise, to read him by
his form, as you are like to find him in the proof of his valour.
He is indeed, sir, the most skilful, bloody, and fatal opposite
that you could possibly have found in any part of Illyria. Will
you walk towards him? I will make your peace with him if
I can.   296

Vio. I shall be much bound to you for't. I am one that had
rather go with sir priest than sir knight. I care not who knows
so much of my mettle.

                                                            Exeunt.

Enter [*Sir*] *Toby* and [*Sir*] *Andrew* [at the orchard end].

To. Why, man, he's a very devil; I have not seen such a
firago. I had a pass with him, rapier, scabbard, and all, and
he gives me the stuck-in with such a mortal motion that it is
inevitable; and on the answer he pays you as surely as your
feet hit the ground they step on. They say he has been fencer
to the Sophy.

And. Pox on't, I'll not meddle with him.

To. Ay, but he will not now be pacified. Fabian can scarce
hold him yonder.   310

And. Plague on't, an I thought he had been valiant, and so
cunning in fence, I'd have seen him damn'd ere I'd have chal-
leng'd him. Let him let the matter slip, and I'll give him my
horse, grey Capilet.   315

To. I'll make the motion. Stand here; make a good show
on't. This shall end without the perdition of souls. [*Aside*]
Marry, I'll ride your horse as well as I ride you.

Enter *Fabian* and *Viola*.

I have his horse to take up the quarrel. I have persuaded him
the youth 's a devil.   321

Fab. He is as horribly conceited of him; and pants and
looks pale, as if a bear were at his heels.   324

To. There's no remedy, sir; he will fight with you for 's
oath sake. Marry, he hath better bethought him of his quarrel,
and he finds that now scarce to be worth talking of. Therefore
draw for the supportance of his vow. He protests he will not
hurt you.   330

Vio. [*aside*] Pray God defend me! A little thing would
make me tell them how much I lack of a man.

Fab. Give ground if you see him furious.   334

To. Come, Sir Andrew, there's no remedy. The gentleman
will for his honour's sake have one bout with you; he cannot
by the duello avoid it; but he has promised me, as he is a
gentleman and a soldier, he will not hurt you. Come on, to't!

And. Pray God he keep his oath!   [*Draws.*]

Enter *Antonio*.

Vio. I do assure you 'tis against my will.   [*Draws.*]

Ant. Put up your sword. If this young gentleman
Have done offence, I take the fault on me;
If you offend him, I for him defy you.   345

To. You, sir? Why, what are you?

Ant. [*draws*] One, sir, that for his love dares yet do more
Than you have heard him brag to you he will.

To. Nay, if you be an undertaker, I am for you. [*Draws.*]

Enter *Officers.*

Fab. O good Sir Toby, hold! Here come the officers.   351

To. [*to Antonio*] I'll be with you anon.

Vio. [*to Sir Andrew*] Pray, sir, put your sword up, if you
please.   355

And. Marry, will I, sir; and for that I promis'd you, I'll be
as good as my word. He will bear you easily, and reins well.

1. Off. This is the man; do thy office.

2. Off. Antonio, I arrest thee at the suit   360
Of Count Orsino.

Ant.   You do mistake me, sir.

1. Off. No, sir, no jot. I know your favour well,
Though now you have no sea-cap on your head.
Take him away. He knows I know him well.

Ant. I must obey. [*To Viola*] This comes with seeking
    you.   366
But there's no remedy; I shall answer it.
What will you do, now my necessity
Makes me to ask you for my purse? It grieves me
Much more for what I cannot do for you   370
Than what befalls myself. You stand amaz'd,
But be of comfort.

2. Off. Come, sir, away.

Ant. I must entreat of you some of that money.

Vio. What money, sir?   375
For the fair kindness you have show'd me here,
And part being prompted by your present trouble,
Out of my lean and low ability
I'll lend you something. My having is not much.

I'll make division of my present with you.			380
Hold, there's half my coffer.

   Ant.				Will you deny me now?
Is't possible that my deserts to you
Can lack persuasion? Do not tempt my misery,
Lest that it make me so unsound a man
As to upbraid you with those kindnesses			385
That I have done for you.

   Vio.				I know of none,
Nor know I you by voice or any feature.
I hate ingratitude more in a man
Than lying, vainness, babbling, drunkenness,
Or any taint of vice whose strong corruption			390
Inhabits our frail blood.

   Ant.				O heavens themselves!

   2. Off. Come, sir, I pray you go.

   Ant. Let me speak a little. This youth that you see here
I snatch'd one half out of the jaws of death;
Reliev'd him with such sanctity of love,			395
And to his image, which methought did promise
Most venerable worth, did I devotion.

   1. Off. What's that to us? The time goes by. Away!

   Ant. But, O, how vile an idol proves this god!
Thou hast, Sebastian, done good feature shame.			400
In nature there's no blemish but the mind;
None can be call'd deform'd but the unkind.
Virtue is beauty; but the beauteous evil
Are empty trunks, o'erflourish'd by the devil.

   1. Off. The man grows mad. Away with him! Come,
    come, sir.					405

   Ant. Lead me on.			*Exit* [*with Officers*].

   Vio. Methinks his words do from such passion fly
That he believes himself; so do not I.

Prove true, imagination, O, prove true,
That I, dear brother, be now ta'en for you!   410

   To. Come hither, knight; come hither, Fabian. We'll whisper o'er a couplet or two of most sage saws.

   Vio. He nam'd Sebastian. I my brother know
Yet living in my glass. Even such and so   415
In favour was my brother, and he went
Still in this fashion, colour, ornament,
For him I imitate. O, if it prove,
Tempests are kind, and salt waves fresh in love!   [*Exit.*]

   To. A very dishonest paltry boy, and more a coward than a hare. His dishonesty appears in leaving his friend here in necessity and denying him; and for his cowardship, ask Fabian.

   Fab. A coward, a most devout coward; religious in it.   425

   And. 'Slid, I'll after him again and beat him!

   To. Do; cuff him soundly, but never draw thy sword.

   And. An I do not—   [*Exit.*]

   Fab. Come, let's see the event.

   To. I dare lay any money 'twill be nothing yet.

       Exeunt.

ACT IV. Scene I. [*Before* Olivia's *house.*]

Enter *Sebastian* and *Clown.*

Clown. Will you make me believe that I am not sent for you?

Seb. Go to, go to, thou art a foolish fellow. Let me be clear of thee. 4

Clown. Well held out, i' faith! No, I do not know you; nor I am not sent to you by my lady, to bid you come speak with her; nor your name is not Master Cesario; nor this is not my nose neither. Nothing that is so is so.

Seb. I prithee vent thy folly somewhere else. Thou know'st not me. 11

Clown. Vent my folly! He has heard that word of some great man, and now applies it to a fool. Vent my folly! I am afraid this great lubber, the world, will prove a cockney. I prithee now, ungird thy strangeness, and tell me what I shall vent to my lady. Shall I vent to her that thou art coming?

Seb. I prithee, foolish Greek, depart from me. There's money for thee. If you tarry longer, 20 I shall give worse payment.

Clown. By my troth, thou hast an open hand. These wise men that give fools money get themselves a good report—after fourteen years' purchase. 25

Enter [*Sir*] *Andrew*, [*Sir*] *Toby*, and *Fabian.*

And. Now, sir, have I met you again? There's for you!
[*Strikes Sebastian.*]

Seb. Why, there's for thee, and there, and there!
[*Strikes Sir Andrew.*]
Are all the people mad?

To. Hold, sir, or I'll throw your dagger o'er the house.
[*Seizes Sebastian.*]

63

Clown. This will I tell my lady straight. I would not be in
some of your coats for two-pence.   [*Exit.*]

To. Come on, sir; hold!   34

And. Nay, let him alone. I'll go another way to work with
him. I'll have an action of battery against him, if there be any
law in Illyria. Though I stroke him first, yet it's no matter
for that.

Seb. Let go thy hand.   40

To. Come, sir, I will not let you go. Come, my young soldier, put up your iron. You are well flesh'd. Come on.

Seb. I will be free from thee. [*Disengages himself.*] What
   wouldst thou now?
If thou dar'st tempt me further, draw thy sword. [*Draws.*] 45

To. What, what? Nay then, I must have an ounce or two
of this malapert blood from you.   [*Draws.*]

Enter *Olivia.*

Oli. Hold, Toby! On thy life I charge thee hold!

To. Madam!   50

Oli. Will it be ever thus? Ungracious wretch,
Fit for the mountains and the barbarous caves,
Where manners ne'er were preach'd! Out of my sight!
Be not offended, dear Cesario.
Rudesby, be gone!
        [*Exeunt Sir Toby, Sir Andrew, and Fabian.*]
                I prithee, gentle friend,   55
Let thy fair wisdom, not thy passion, sway
In this uncivil and unjust extent
Against thy peace. Go with me to my house,
And hear thou there how many fruitless pranks
This ruffian hath botch'd up, that thou thereby   60
Mayst smile at this. Thou shalt not choose but go;

Do not deny. Beshrew his soul for me!
He started one poor heart of mine, in thee.
  Seb. What relish is in this? How runs the stream?
Or I am mad, or else this is a dream.   65
Let fancy still my sense in Lethe steep;
If it be thus to dream, still let me sleep!
  Oli. Nay, come, I prithee. Would thou'dst be rul'd by me!
  Seb. Madam, I will.
  Oli.   O, say so, and so be!

                               Exeunt.

Scene II. [Olivia's *house*.]

Enter *Maria* and *Clown*.

  Mar. Nay, I prithee put on this gown and this beard; make
him believe thou art Sir Topas the curate; do it quickly. I'll
call Sir Toby the whilst.   [*Exit.*]
  Clown. Well, I'll put it on, and I will dissemble myself in't,
and I would I were the first that ever dissembled in such a
gown. I am not tall enough to become the function well, nor
lean enough to be thought a good student; but to be said an
honest man and a good housekeeper goes as fairly as to say a
careful man and a great scholar. The competitors enter.   12

Enter [*Sir*] *Toby* [and *Maria*].

  To. Jove bless thee, Master Parson.
  Clown. Bonos dies, Sir Toby; for, as the old hermit of
Prague, that never saw pen and ink, very wittily said to a niece
of King Gorboduc, 'That that is is'; so I, being Master Parson,
am Master Parson; for what is 'that' but that, and 'is' but is?
  To. To him, Sir Topas.   20
  Clown. What ho, I say. Peace in this prison!
  To. The knave counterfeits well; a good knave.

Malvolio within.

Mal. Who calls there?

Clown. Sir Topas the curate, who comes to visit Malvolio
the lunatic. 26

Mal. Sir Topas, Sir Topas, good Sir Topas, go to my lady.

Clown. Out, hyperbolical fiend! How vexest thou this man!
Talkest thou nothing but of ladies? 30

To. Well said, Master Parson.

Mal. Sir Topas, never was man thus wronged. Good Sir
Topas, do not think I am mad. They have laid me here in
hideous darkness. 34

Clown. Fie, thou dishonest Satan! I call thee by the most
modest terms; for I am one of those gentle ones that will
use the devil himself with courtesy. Say'st thou that house
is dark?

Mal. As hell, Sir Topas. 39

Clown. Why, it hath·bay windows transparent as barricadoes, and the clerestories toward the south north are as lustrous
as ebony; and yet complainest thou of obstruction?

Mal. I am not mad, Sir Topas. I say to you this house is
dark. 45

Clown. Madman, thou errest. I say there is no darkness but
ignorance, in which thou art more puzzled than the Egyptians
in their fog.

Mal. I say this house is as dark as ignorance, though ignorance were as dark as hell; and I say there was never man
thus abus'd. I am no more mad than you are. Make the trial
of it in any constant question.

Clown. What is the opinion of Pythagoras concerning wild
fowl? 55

Mal. That the soul of our grandam might happily inhabit
a bird.

Clown. What think'st thou of his opinion?

Mal. I think nobly of the soul and no way approve his
opinion.   60

Clown. Fare thee well. Remain thou still in darkness. Thou
shalt hold th' opinion of Pythagoras ere I will allow of thy
wits, and fear to kill a woodcock, lest thou dispossess the soul
of thy grandam. Fare thee well.   65

Mal. Sir Topas, Sir Topas!

To. My most exquisite Sir Topas!

Clown. Nay, I am for all waters.

Mar. Thou mightst have done this without thy beard and
gown. He sees thee not.   70

To. To him in thine own voice, and bring me word how
thou find'st him.—[*To Maria*] I would we were well rid of
this knavery. If he may be conveniently deliver'd, I would he
were; for I am now so far in offence with my niece that I cannot pursue with any safety this sport to the upshot.—[*To
the Clown*] Come by-and-by to my chamber.

                                                        Exit [*with Maria*].

Clown. [*sings*] 'Hey, Robin, jolly Robin,
                              Tell me how thy lady does.'

Mal. Fool!   80

Clown. 'My lady is unkind, perdie!'

Mal. Fool!

Clown. 'Alas, why is she so?'

Mal. Fool, I say!

Clown. 'She loves another'—Who calls, ha?   85

Mal. Good fool, as ever thou wilt deserve well at my hand,
help me to a candle, and pen, ink, and paper. As I am a gentleman, I will live to be thankful to thee for't.

Clown. Master Malvolio?   90

Mal. Ay, good fool.

Clown. Alas, sir, how fell you besides your five wits?

Mal. Fool, there was never man so notoriously abus'd. I am
as well in my wits, fool, as thou art.   96

Clown. But as well? Then you are mad indeed, if you be
no better in your wits than a fool.

Mal. They have here propertied me; keep me in darkness,
send ministers to me, asses, and do all they can to face me out
of my wits.   101

Clown. Advise you what you say. The minister is here.—
Malvolio, Malvolio, thy wits the heavens restore! Endeavour
thyself to sleep and leave thy vain bibble babble.   105

Mal. Sir Topas!

Clown. Maintain no words with him, good fellow.—Who,
I, sir? Not I, sir. God b' wi' you, good Sir Topas!—Marry,
amen.—I will, sir, I will.

Mal. Fool, fool, fool, I say!   110

Clown. Alas, sir, be patient. What say you, sir? I am shent
for speaking to you.

Mal. Good fool, help me to some light and some paper. I
tell thee, I am as well in my wits as any man in Illyria. 115

Clown. Well-a-day that you were, sir!

Mal. By this hand, I am. Good fool, some ink, paper, and
light; and convey what I will set down to my lady. It shall
advantage thee more than ever the bearing of letter did. 120

Clown. I will help you to't. But tell me true, are you not
mad indeed? or do you but counterfeit?

Mal. Believe me, I am not. I tell thee true.

Clown. Nay, I'll ne'er believe a madman till I see his brains.
I will fetch you light and paper and ink.   127

Mal. Fool, I'll requite it in the highest degree. I prithee be
gone.

Clown. [*sings*]   I am gone, sir;   130
                      And anon, sir,
                      I'll be with you again,

                                    In a trice,
                                Like to the old Vice,
                             Your need to sustain;   135
                             Who, with dagger of lath,
                             In his rage and his wrath,
                                Cries 'aha!' to the devil.
                             Like a mad lad,
                             'Pare thy nails, dad.'   140
                                Adieu, goodman devil.   *Exit.*

                    Scene III. [Olivia's *orchard*.]

                          Enter *Sebastian*.

Seb. This is the air; that is the glorious sun;
This pearl she gave me, I do feel't and see't;
And though 'tis wonder that enwraps me thus,
Yet 'tis not madness. Where's Antonio then?
I could not find him at the Elephant;   5
Yet there he was; and there I found this credit,
That he did range the town to seek me out.
His counsel now might do me golden service;
For though my soul disputes well with my sense
That this may be some error, but no madness,   10
Yet doth this accident and flood of fortune
So far exceed all instance, all discourse,
That I am ready to distrust mine eyes
And wrangle with my reason, that persuades me
To any other trust but that I am mad,   15
Or else the lady 's mad. Yet, if 'twere so,
She could not sway her house, command her followers,
Take and give back affairs and their dispatch
With such a smooth, discreet, and stable bearing

As I perceive she does. There's something in't   20
That is deceivable. But here the lady comes.

Enter *Olivia* and *Priest*.

    Oli. Blame not this haste of mine. If you mean well,
Now go with me and with this holy man
Into the chantry by. There, before him,
And underneath that consecrated roof,   25
Plight me the full assurance of your faith,
That my most jealous and too doubtful soul
May live at peace. He shall conceal it
Whiles you are willing it shall come to note,
What time we will our celebration keep   30
According to my birth. What do you say?

    Seb. I'll follow this good man and go with you
And having sworn truth, ever will be true.

    Oli. Then lead the way, good father; and heavens so shine
That they may fairly note this act of mine!   35

                                                               Exeunt.

ACT V. Scene I. [*Before* Olivia's *house*.]

Enter *Clown* and *Fabian*.

Fab. Now as thou lov'st me, let me see his letter.
Clown. Good Master Fabian, grant me another request.
Fab. Anything.   5
Clown. Do not desire to see this letter.
Fab. This is to give a dog, and in recompense desire my dog again.

Enter *Duke, Viola, Curio,* and *Lords.*

Duke. Belong you to the Lady Olivia, friends?
Clown. Ay, sir, we are some of her trappings.   10
Duke. I know thee well. How dost thou, my good fellow?
Clown. Truly, sir, the better for my foes, and the worse for my friends.
Duke. Just the contrary: the better for thy friends.   16
Clown. No, sir, the worse.
Duke. How can that be?
Clown. Marry, sir, they praise me and make an ass of me. Now my foes tell me plainly I am an ass; so that by my foes, sir, I profit in the knowledge of myself, and by my friends I am abused; so that, conclusions to be as kisses, if your four negatives make your two affirmatives, why then, the worse for my friends and the better for my foes.   26
Duke. Why, this is excellent.
Clown. By my troth, sir, no; though it please you to be one of my friends.   30
Duke. Thou shalt not be the worse for me. There's gold.
Clown. But that it would be double-dealing, sir, I would you could make it another.
Duke. O, you give me ill counsel.

Clown. Put your grace in your pocket, sir, for this once, and let your flesh and blood obey it.   36

Duke. Well, I will be so much a sinner to be a double-dealer. There's another.

Clown. Primo, secundo, tertio is a good play; and the old saying is 'The third pays for all.' The triplex, sir, is a good tripping measure; or the bells of Saint Bennet, sir, may put you in mind—one, two, three.   43

Duke. You can fool no more money out of me at this throw. If you will let your lady know I am here to speak with her, and bring her along with you, it may awake my bounty further.

Clown. Marry, sir, lullaby to your bounty till I come again! I go, sir; but I would not have you to think that my desire of having is the sin of covetousness. But, as you say, sir, let your bounty take a nap; I will awake it anon.   *Exit.*

Enter *Antonio* and *Officers*.

Vio. Here comes the man, sir, that did rescue me.

Duke. That face of his I do remember well;
Yet when I saw it last, it was besmear'd   55
As black as Vulcan in the smoke of war.
A baubling vessel was he captain of,
For shallow draught and bulk unprizable,
With which such scathful grapple did he make
With the most noble bottom of our fleet   60
That very envy and the tongue of loss
Cried fame and honour on him. What's the matter?

1. Off. Orsino, this is that Antonio
That took the Phœnix and her fraught from Candy;
And this is he that did the Tiger board   65
When your young nephew Titus lost his leg.
Here in the streets, desperate of shame and state,
In private brabble did we apprehend him.

Vio. He did me kindness, sir; drew on my side;
But in conclusion put strange speech upon me.   70
I know not what 'twas but distraction.
  Duke. Notable pirate, thou salt-water thief!
What foolish boldness brought thee to their mercies
Whom thou in terms so bloody and so dear
Hast made thine enemies?
  Ant.   Orsino, noble sir,   75
Be pleas'd that I shake off these names you give me.
Antonio never yet was thief or pirate,
Though I confess, on base and ground enough,
Orsino's enemy. A witchcraft drew me hither.
That most ingrateful boy there by your side   80
From the rude sea's enrag'd and foamy mouth
Did I redeem. A wrack past hope he was.
His life I gave him, and did thereto add
My love without retention or restraint,
All his in dedication. For his sake   85
Did I expose myself (pure for his love)
Into the danger of this adverse town;
Drew to defend him when he was beset;
Where being apprehended, his false cunning
(Not meaning to partake with me in danger)   90
Taught him to face me out of his acquaintance,
And grew a twenty years removed thing
While one would wink; denied me mine own purse,
Which I had recommended to his use
Not half an hour before.
  Vio.   How can this be?   95
  Duke. When came he to this town?
  Ant. To-day, my lord; and for three months before,
No int'rim, not a minute's vacancy,
Both day and night did we keep company.

Enter *Olivia* and *Attendants*.

Duke. Here comes the Countess; now heaven walks on
earth.   100
But for thee, fellow—fellow, thy words are madness.
Three months this youth hath tended upon me;
But more of that anon. Take him aside.

Oli. What would my lord, but that he may not have,
Wherein Olivia may seem serviceable?   105
Cesario, you do not keep promise with me.

Vio. Madam!

Duke. Gracious Olivia—

Oli. What do you say, Cesario?—Good my lord—

Vio. My lord would speak; my duty hushes me.   110

Oli. If it be aught to the old tune, my lord,
It is as fat and fulsome to mine ear
As howling after music.

Duke.   Still so cruel?

Oli. Still so constant, lord.

Duke. What, to perverseness? You uncivil lady,   115
To whose ingrate and unauspicious altars
My soul the faithfull'st off'rings hath breath'd out
That e'er devotion tender'd! What shall I do?

Oli. Even what it please my lord, that shall become him.

Duke. Why should I not, had I the heart to do it,   120
Like to th' Egyptian thief at point of death,
Kill what I love?—a savage jealousy
That sometime savours nobly. But hear me this:
Since you to non-regardance cast my faith,
And that I partly know the instrument   125
That screws me from my true place in your favour,
Live you the marble-breasted tyrant still.
But this your minion, whom I know you love,

And whom, by heaven I swear, I tender dearly,
Him will I tear out of that cruel eye   130
Where he sits crowned in his master's spite.
Come, boy, with me. My thoughts are ripe in mischief.
I'll sacrifice the lamb that I do love
To spite a raven's heart within a dove.   [*Going.*]
  Vio. And I, most jocund, apt, and willingly,   135
To do you rest a thousand deaths would die.   [*Following.*]
  Oli. Where goes Cesario?
  Vio.   After him I love
More than I love these eyes, more than my life,
More, by all mores, than e'er I shall love wife.
If I do feign, you witnesses above   140
Punish my life for tainting of my love!
  Oli. Ay me detested! how am I beguil'd!
  Vio. Who does beguile you? Who does do you wrong?
  Oli. Hast thou forgot thyself? Is it so long?
Call forth the holy father.   [*Exit an Attendant.*]
  Duke.   [*to Viola*] Come, away!   145
  Oli. Whither, my lord? Cesario, husband, stay.
  Duke. Husband?
  Oli.   Ay, husband. Can he that deny?
  Duke. Her husband, sirrah?
  Vio.   No, my lord, not I.
  Oli. Alas, it is the baseness of thy fear
That makes thee strangle thy propriety.   150
Fear not, Cesario; take thy fortunes up;
Be that thou know'st thou art, and then thou art
As great as that thou fear'st.

Enter *Priest*.

                O, welcome, father!
Father, I charge thee by thy reverence

Here to unfold—though lately we intended   155
To keep in darkness what occasion now
Reveals before 'tis ripe—what thou dost know
Hath newly pass'd between this youth and me.

   Priest. A contract of eternal bond of love,
Confirm'd by mutual joinder of your hands,   160
Attested by the holy close of lips,
Strength'ned by interchangement of your rings;
And all the ceremony of this compact
Seal'd in my function, by my testimony;
Since when, my watch hath told me, toward my grave   165
I have travell'd but two hours.

   Duke. O thou dissembling cub! What wilt thou be
When time hath sow'd a grizzle on thy case?
Or will not else thy craft so quickly grow
That thine own trip shall be thine overthrow?   170
Farewell, and take her; but direct thy feet
Where thou and I, henceforth, may never meet.

   Vio. My lord, I do protest—

   Oli.   O, do not swear!
Hold little faith, though thou hast too much fear.

               Enter *Sir Andrew.*

   And. For the love of God, a surgeon! Send one presently
to Sir Toby.   176

   Oli. What's the matter?

   And. Has broke my head across, and has given Sir Toby a
bloody coxcomb too. For the love of God, your help! I had
rather than forty pound I were at home.   181

   Oli. Who has done this, Sir Andrew?

   And. The Count's gentleman, one Cesario. We took him
for a coward, but he's the very devil incardinate.   185

   Duke. My gentleman Cesario?

SPIRITUAL NOBILITY OF CHARACTER

And. Od's lifelings, here he is! You broke my head for
nothing; and that that I did, I was set on to do't by Sir Toby.

Vio. Why do you speak to me? I never hurt you.   190
You drew your sword upon me without cause,
But I bespake you fair and hurt you not.

Enter [*Sir*] *Toby* and *Clown.*

And. If a bloody coxcomb be a hurt, you have hurt me. I
think you set nothing by a bloody coxcomb. Here comes Sir
Toby halting—you shall hear more. But if he had not been
in drink, he would have tickled you othergates than he did.

Duke. How now, gentleman? How is't with you?   200

To. That's all one! Has hurt me, and there's th' end on't.—
Sot, didst see Dick Surgeon, sot?

Clown. O, he's drunk, Sir Toby, an hour agone. His eyes
were set at eight i' th' morning.

To. Then he's a rogue and a passy measures pavin. I hate a
drunken rogue.   207

Oli. Away with him! Who hath made this havoc with
them?

And. I'll help you, Sir Toby, because we'll be dress'd together.   211

To. Will you help—an ass-head and a coxcomb and a knave
—a thin-fac'd knave, a gull?

Oli. Get him to bed, and let his hurt be look'd to.   215
        [*Exeunt Clown, Fabian, Sir Toby, and Sir Andrew.*]

Enter *Sebastian.*

Seb. I am sorry, madam, I have hurt your kinsman;
But had it been the brother of my blood,
I must have done no less with wit and safety.
You throw a strange regard upon me, and by that

I do perceive it hath offended you. 220
Pardon me, sweet one, even for the vows
We made each other but so late ago.

Duke. One face, one voice, one habit, and two persons!
A natural perspective, that is and is not!

Seb. Antonio! O my dear Antonio! 225
How have the hours rack'd and tortur'd me
Since I have lost thee!

Ant. Sebastian are you?

Seb.   Fear'st thou that, Antonio?

Ant. How have you made division of yourself?
An apple cleft in two is not more twin 230
Than these two creatures. Which is Sebastian?

Oli. Most wonderful!

Seb. Do I stand there? I never had a brother;
Nor can there be that deity in my nature
Of here and everywhere. I had a sister, 235
Whom the blind waves and surges have devour'd.
Of charity, what kin are you to me?
What countryman? what name? what parentage?

Vio. Of Messaline; Sebastian was my father—
Such a Sebastian was my brother too; 240
So went he suited to his watery tomb.
If spirits can assume both form and suit,
You come to fright us.

Seb.   A spirit I am indeed,
But am in that dimension grossly clad
Which from the womb I did participate. 245
Were you a woman, as the rest goes even,
I should my tears let fall upon your cheek
And say, 'Thrice welcome, drowned Viola!'

Vio. My father had a mole upon his brow—

Seb. And so had mine. 250

  Vio. And died that day when Viola from her birth
Had numb'red thirteen years.
  Seb. O, that record is lively in my soul!
He finished indeed his mortal act
That day that made my sister thirteen years.   255
  Vio. If nothing lets to make us happy both
But this my masculine usurp'd attire,
Do not embrace me till each circumstance
Of place, time, fortune do cohere and jump
That I am Viola; which to confirm,   260
I'll bring you to a captain in this town,
Where lie my maiden weeds; by whose gentle help
I was preserv'd to serve this noble Count.
All the occurrence of my fortune since
Hath been between this lady and this lord.   265
  Seb. [*to Olivia*] So comes it, lady, you have been mistook.
But nature to her bias drew in that.
You would have been contracted to a maid;
Nor are you therein, by my life, deceiv'd:
You are betroth'd both to a maid and man.   270
  Duke. Be not amaz'd; right noble is his blood.
If this be so, as yet the glass seems true,
I shall have share in this most happy wrack.
[*To Viola*] Boy, thou hast said to me a thousand times
Thou never shouldst love woman like to me.   275
  Vio. And all those sayings will I over swear,
And all those swearings keep as true in soul
As doth that orbed continent the fire
That severs day from night.
  Duke.   Give me thy hand,
And let me see thee in thy woman's weeds.   280
  Vio. The captain that did bring me first on shore
Hath my maid's garments. He upon some action

Is now in durance, at Malvolio's suit,
A gentleman, and follower of my lady's.

Oli. He shall enlarge him. Fetch Malvolio hither.   285
And yet alas! now I remember me,
They say, poor gentleman, he's much distract.

Enter *Clown* with a letter, and *Fabian*.

A most extracting frenzy of mine own
From my remembrance clearly banish'd his.
How does he, sirrah?   290

Clown. Truly, madam, he holds Belzebub at the stave's end
as well as a man in his case may do. Has here writ a letter to
you; I should have given't you to-day morning. [*Offers the
letter.*] But as a madman's epistles are no gospels, so it skills
not much when they are deliver'd.   296

Oli. Open't and read it.

Clown. Look then to be well edified, when the fool delivers
the madman. [*Reads in a loud voice*] 'By the Lord, madam'—

Oli. How now? Art thou mad?   301

Clown. No, madam, I do but read madness. An your ladyship will have it as it ought to be, you must allow vox.

Oli. Prithee read i' thy right wits.   305

Clown. So I do, madonna; but to read his right wits is to
read thus. Therefore perpend, my princess, and give ear.

Oli. [*to Fabian*] Read it you, sirrah.   309

Fab. (*reads*) 'By the Lord, madam, you wrong me, and the
world shall know it. Though you have put me into darkness, and
given your drunken cousin rule over me, yet have I the benefit of my
senses as well as your ladyship. I have your own letter that induced
me to the semblance I put on; with the which I doubt not but to do
myself much right, or you much shame. Think of me as you please.
I leave my duty a little unthought of, and speak out of my injury.

                         'THE MADLY US'D MALVOLIO.'

Oli. Did he write this? 320
Clown. Ay, madam.
Duke. This savours not much of distraction.
Oli. See him deliver'd, Fabian; bring him hither.

[*Exit Fabian.*]

My lord, so please you, these things further thought on,
To think me as well a sister as a wife, 325
One day shall crown th' alliance on't, so please you,
Here at my house and at my proper cost.
    Duke. Madam, I am most apt t' embrace your offer.
[*To Viola*] Your master quits you; and for your service done him,
So much against the mettle of your sex, 330
So far beneath your soft and tender breeding,
And since you call'd me master, for so long,
Here is my hand: you shall from this time be
Your master's mistress.
    Oli.   A sister! you are she.

Enter [*Fabian, with*] Malvolio.

Duke. Is this the madman?
    Oli.   Ay, my lord, this same. 335
How now, Malvolio?
    Mal.   Madam, you have done me wrong,
Notorious wrong.
    Oli.   Have I, Malvolio? No.
    Mal. Lady, you have. Pray you peruse that letter.
You must not now deny it is your hand.
Write from it if you can, in hand or phrase, 340
Or say 'tis not your seal, not your invention.
You can say none of this. Well, grant it then,
And tell me, in the modesty of honour,
Why you have given me such clear lights of favour,

Bade me come smiling and cross-garter'd to you,   345
To put on yellow stockings, and to frown
Upon Sir Toby and the lighter people;
And, acting this in an obedient hope,
Why have you suffer'd me to be imprison'd,
Kept in a dark house, visited by the priest,   350
And made the most notorious geck and gull
That e'er invention play'd on? Tell me why.

    Oli. Alas, Malvolio, this is not my writing,
Though I confess much like the character;
But, out of question, 'tis Maria's hand.   355
And now I do bethink me, it was she
First told me thou wast mad. Thou cam'st in smiling,
And in such forms which here were presuppos'd
Upon thee in the letter. Prithee be content.
This practice hath most shrewdly pass'd upon thee;   360
But when we know the grounds and authors of it,
Thou shalt be both the plaintiff and the judge
Of thine own cause.

    Fab.   Good madam, hear me speak,
And let no quarrel, nor no brawl to come,
Taint the condition of this present hour,   365
Which I have wond'red at. In hope it shall not,
Most freely I confess myself and Toby
Set this device against Malvolio here,
Upon some stubborn and uncourteous parts
We had conceiv'd against him. Maria writ   370
The letter, at Sir Toby's great importance,
In recompense whereof he hath married her.
How with a sportful malice it was follow'd
May rather pluck on laughter than revenge,
If that the injuries be justly weigh'd   375
That have on both sides pass'd.

Oli. Alas poor fool, how have they baffled thee!   maximic

Clown. Why, 'some are born great, some achieve greatness, and some have greatness thrown upon them.' I was one, sir, in this interlude—one Sir Topas, sir; but that's all one. 'By the Lord, fool, I am not mad!' But do you remember— 'Madam, why laugh you at such a barren rascal? An you smile not, he's gagg'd'? And thus the whirligig of time brings in his revenges.   385

Mal. I'll be reveng'd on the whole pack of you!   [*Exit.*]

Oli. He hath been most notoriously abus'd.

Duke. Pursue him and entreat him to a peace.
He hath not told us of the captain yet.   390
When that is known, and golden time convents,
A solemn combination shall be made
Of our dear souls. Meantime, sweet sister,
We will not part from hence. Cesario, come—
For so you shall be while you are a man;   395
But when in other habits you are seen,
Orsino's mistress and his fancy's queen.

                            Exeunt [*all but the Clown*].

                    Clown sings.

    When that I was and a little tiny boy,
        With hey, ho, the wind and the rain,
    A foolish thing was but a toy,   400
        For the rain it raineth every day.

    But when I came to man's estate,
        With hey, ho, the wind and the rain,
    'Gainst knaves and thieves men shut their gate,
        For the rain it raineth every day.   405

    But when I came, alas! to wive,
        With hey, ho, the wind and the rain,

By swaggering could I never thrive,
　For the rain it raineth every day.

But when I came unto my beds,　　　　　　410
　With hey, ho, the wind and the rain,
With tosspots still had drunken heads,
　For the rain it raineth every day.

A great while ago the world begun,
　With hey, ho, the wind and the rain;　　415
But that's all one, our play is done,
　And we'll strive to please you every day.

[*Exit.*]

NOTES

1-3. If music be the food of love, play on, etc. If music is food for love, play on, until love's appetite for music is fully satisfied. Cf. *Antony and Cleopatra*, ii, 5, 1, 2: 'Give me some music! music, moody food Of us that trade in love' (Wright). Note also Orsino's words in ii, 4, 1-4.—**sicken.** We note that the 'excess' that cloys love's appetite for music comes almost instantly (ll. 7, 8).

4. fall: cadence.

5-7. it came . . . odour! It charmed my ear with a sound as soothing as the pleasant murmur of the wind that brings with it the sweetness of the violets growing upon some bank upon which it has breathed and from which it has stolen the perfume it brings. *Sound* is a word applicable both to music and to the wind, and *sweet* is applicable both to sounds and to odours. Orsino is playing delicately with words, and his language should not be judged as if he were composing a treatise on meteorology. Yet many critics have objected to the reading 'sound.' Rowe substitutes 'wind' and Pope 'south.'[1] Wilson is favourably disposed toward the anonymous conjecture 'sough.'

9-13. how quick and fresh: how keenly alive to new thoughts and notions.—**That:** in that; inasmuch as.—**capacity:** receptive power. Used in a more active sense than in modern English.—**as the sea.** Cf. ii, 4, 103: 'as hungry as the sea'; *Tempest*, iii, 3,

---

[1] *South* is, at first sight, an attractive reading, but (as Knight remarks) Shakespeare's references to the south wind are quite out of accord with the present passage. See *As You Like It*, iii, 5, 50: 'Like foggy south, puffing with wind and rain.' Cf. 2 *Henry IV*, ii, 4, 392-394; *Romeo and Juliet*, i, 4, 103; *Cymbeline*, ii, 3, 136. Note, however, Marston, *Antonio and Mellida*, i, 1, 154, 155 (ed. Bullen, I, 24): 'Smile heaven, and softest southern wind Kiss her cheek gently with perfumed breath!'

55: 'the never-surfeited sea.'—**naught enters there . . . minute:** every new idea that enters the lover's mind—however highly he regards it at first—loses its value in a minute. The grammatical antecedent of *there* is *capacity.*—**Of what validity and pitch soe'er:** of whatsoever value; however valuable and highly esteemed. *Validity* and *pitch* are synonymous. *Pitch* is the regular term for the height reached by a soaring falcon. It is often used metaphorically. Cf. *Richard III*, iii, 7, 188: 'the pitch and height of his degree.'—**abatement:** reduction in value.

14, 15. **So full of shapes is fancy . . . fantastical:** Fancy (i.e., love, the lover's brain) is so 'full of shapes' (figures of the imagination) that—though limitless in its capacity (its ability to take them in)—it soon tires of each and every one of them (cf. ii, 4, 17–20). Thus we may truly say that love is the one quality in human nature that is 'high fantastical'—imaginative in the highest degree. Cf. *Midsummer Night's Dream*, v, 1, 7, 8:

> The lunatic, the lover, and the poet
> Are of imagination all compact.

For *fancy* cf. ii, 4, 34; v, 1, 397.

21. **a hart.** The story of Actæon, transformed by Diana to a stag because he had seen her bathing (Ovid, *Metamorphoses*, iii, 138 ff.), was familiar to every reader. See *Titus Andronicus*, ii, 3, 61–71; *Merry Wives*, ii, 1, 122; iii, 2, 44. Actæon 'represents a man who, indulging his eyes, or his imagination, with the view of a woman that he cannot gain, has his heart torn with incessant longing' (Johnson).

22. **fell:** fierce.

24. **So please my lord.** Literally, 'so may it please'; but used like *if you please* (i.e., if it be pleasing to you) as a courteous formula of submission or apology.

26. **The element:** the sky; the heavens. Cf. *Julius Cæsar*, i, 3, 128–130:

The complexion of the element
In favour 's [i.e., in appearance is] like the work we have in hand,
Most bloody, fiery, and most terrible.

—**heat:** course.

28. **like a cloistress:** as if her chamber were a cloister and she
a nun.

30–32. **eye-offending brine.** That tears are salt, that they
irritate the eyes, and that salt is a preservative, are facts which
Shakespeare kept vividly in mind. Cf. *All's Well*, i, 1, 53–56:

> *Lafeu.* Your commendations, madam, get from her tears.
> *Countess.* 'Tis the best brine a maiden can season her praise in;

Romeo and Juliet, ii, 3, 69–72:

> What a deal of brine
> Hath wash'd thy sallow cheeks for Rosaline!
> How much salt water thrown away in waste,
> To season love!

Hamlet, i, 2, 154, 155:

> Ere yet the salt of most unrighteous tears
> Had left the flushing in her galled eyes.

—**to season A brother's dead love:** to preserve her love for a
dead brother.—**remembrance.** Quadrisyllabic—*rememberance*.

35. **golden shaft.** Cupid has two arrows: one (tipped with
gold) causes love; the other (tipped with lead) causes indiffer-
ence or aversion. See Ovid, *Metamorphoses*, i, 468–471. Cf.
Midsummer Night's Dream, i, 1, 169, 170:

> I swear to thee by Cupid's strongest bow,
> By his best arrow, with the golden head.

Lyly treats the subject of Cupid's arrows with elaboration in his
Sapho and Phao, v, 1 and 2.

36. **all affections else:** all other thoughts, emotions, and feelings.

37–39. when liver ... king! when her liver (the seat of the passion of love),[1] her brain (the organ of thought), and her heart (the organ of emotion)—these thrones which sway her nature[2]—are all three filled (to the exclusion of every other thought or feeling) with passionate love for one and the same person. Cf. Coleridge, *Love*:

> All thoughts, all passions, all delights,
> Whatever stirs this mortal frame,
> All are but ministers of Love,
> And feed his sacred flame.

—supplied and fill'd. Synonymous.—**Her sweet perfections.** In apposition with 'liver, brain, and heart.' Cf. i, 5, 315.

41. rich: as if in a chamber adorned with splendid tapestry hangings. Cf. *2 Henry VI*, v, 3, 12.

Scene II.

---

4. Elysium: heaven. The selection of a word that resembles *Illyria* is manifestly intentional.

6. perchance. Spoken with emphasis on *-chance*: 'It is by mere *chance*.'

11. driving: drifting; driving before the wind.

13. the practice: the plan; the method of procedure.

14. liv'd: floated unsubmerged.

15. like Arion. According to the ancient story the bard Arion, on a voyage from Sicily to Corinth, sprang overboard to escape from the sailors, who were about to murder him for his treasures. He was rescued by a dolphin, which had been enchanted by his

[1] Cf. ii, 4, 101; ii, 5, 106; iii, 2, 21.
[2] Cf. *Cymbeline*, v, 5, 14, 15: 'To you, the liver, heart, and brain of Britain, By whom (I grant) she lives.'

music. Riding on the dolphin's back, he sang and played on his lyre. The waves grew calm at the sound, and Arion was carried ashore in safety. See Herodotus, i, 24; Ovid, *Fasti*, ii, 83 ff. The present passage is almost a translation from Ovid (ii, 113–116):

> Tergo delphina recurvo
> se memorant oneri supposuisse novo.
> Ille sedens citharamque tenet, pretiumque vehendi,
> cantat et aequoreas carmine mulcet aquas.

Arion 'ryding alofte vpon hiz olld freend the Dolphin (that from hed to tayl waz a foour & twenty foot long' was a feature of the entertainment offered to Queen Elizabeth by Leicester at Kenilworth in 1575 (Robert Laneham's Letter, ed. Furnivall, p. 34). Cf. *Midsummer Night's Dream*, ii, 1, 150, and note.

16. **hold acquaintance with the waves**: i.e., rise and fall with them without being overwhelmed.

19, 20. **unfoldeth**: reveals.—**Whereto . . . authority**: which what you have just said suffices to justify.

21. **country**. Trisyllabic. Cf. i, l, 32 (*remembrance*).

22. **bred**: begotten.

32. **as**: as [it naturally would be, for]. This use of *as* in ellipsis is an old idiom. Cf. iii, 4, 212; v, 1, 246, 272.

40. **abjur'd**. Used in the full sense of the word—'renounced by a solemn vow.' See i, 1, 26–32.

42–44. **delivered**: reported, revealed.—**Till . . . mellow**: 'till I had myself provided a fit occasion' (Child).—**estate**: rank; station in life. Cf. i, 3, 117; i, 5, 297.

44–46. **to compass**: to bring about; to effect.—**not**: not even.

48. **though that**. Particles and relative adverbs are often reinforced by the addition of *that*: *if that*, *though that*, *since that*, *lest that*, *when that*, etc. Cf. i, 5, 324; iii, 4, 384; v, 1, 375.

51. **character**: appearance.

54. **haply shall become**: perchance will suit.

56. eunuch. This particular feature of Viola's plan seems to have been dropped. It is never referred to again.

59. allow me . . . service: cause me to be approved by him as very worthy to be taken into his service.

60, 61. What: whatever.—**Only . . . wit:** All I ask of you is to consent to my plan and then to keep silence, leaving it to my skill to carry it out successfully.—**to:** in accordance with.

62. mute: dumb attendant; silent accomplice. Cf. *Cymbeline*, iii, 5, 158, 159: 'a voluntary mute to my design.'

63. When my tongue . . . see: If I prove a blabber, let my eyes be smitten with blindness!

Scene III.

3–5. By my troth: literally, 'by my pledged faith.'—**cousin:** niece. *Cousin* was a word of varied application—cousin, uncle or aunt, nephew or niece. Cf. i, 5, 131.

7. except before excepted! A law phrase providing for exceptions in a lease or other grant: 'the matters previously excepted being excepted,' 'except for the exceptions already made,' 'with all necessary exceptions,' 'exceptis excipiendis.' Sir Toby echoes Maria's word *exceptions* (i.e., objections) and applies the law phrase in a new sense: 'Let her take exception to my conduct as much as she likes! What do I care?'

8, 9. modest: moderate.—**order:** orderly conduct; good behaviour.

10–12. confine myself: clothe myself.—**be.** A good old plural.—**An:** if.—**hang . . . straps.** Cf. *1 Henry IV*, ii, 2, 46, 47: 'Go hang thyself in thine own heir-apparent garters!' See Tilley, *Philological Quarterly*, VI (1927), 307.

13. will undo you: will be your ruin.

20. tall: sturdy and valiant. Thus the audience is led to expect a very different figure from the spindle-shanked Sir Andrew who enters at l. 46. Cf. *Merry Wives*, ii, 2, 12: 'good soldiers and tall fellows.'

22. **ducats.** The ducat was an Italian coin worth, in Shakespeare's time, about four or five shillings.

27. **viol-de-gamboys:** a kind of bass viol—Italian *viola da gamba* ('viol for the leg'), so called 'because men hold it betweene or vpon their legges' (Florio, *Queen Anna's New World of Words*, 1611, p. 602; quoted by Wright).

28, 29. **word . . . book.** The suggestion is that Sir Andrew had learned a number of phrases by heart and can speak them off glibly without referring to the phrase-book. He uses a little French (iii, 1, 78), but does not know what *pourquoi* means (i, 3, 96).

30–33. **almost natural:** almost like a natural—i.e., a born fool, an idiot.—**the gust . . . in:** his taste for; his fondness for.—**the prudent:** the foreseeing; those who have the gift of foresight.

36. **substractors:** for *subtractors*—i.e., persons who maliciously *take away* one's actual merits; slanderers.

44. **coystrill:** base fellow. A coystrill is, literally, a groom who takes care of a knight's horses.

45. **a parish top.** 'A large top was formerly kept in every village, to be whipped in frosty weather, that the peasants might be kept warm by exercise, and out of mischief, while they could not work' (Steevens).—**wench:** girl—merely a familiar term, with no special significance. Cf. ii, 3, 194; ii, 5, 120, 199.

46. **Castiliano vulgo.** The exact sense is beyond reasonable conjecture. Obviously Sir Toby means to exhort Maria to receive Sir Andrew with decorum and not to make open fun of him as she might be tempted to do. The Castilians (Spaniards) were proverbially grave and ceremonious. Warburton and Hanmer emend to 'Castiliano volto'—i.e., 'a Castilian countenance.'—**Agueface.** Sir Andrew, as his name Aguecheek implies,

is pale and 'thin-faced' (v, 1, 213), like a man who suffers from 'fever and ague'—malarial fever—an ailment very common in England in Shakespeare's time on account of the undrained marshes. Cf. *King John*, iii, 4, 84, 85:

> And he will look as hollow as a ghost,
> As dim and meagre as an ague's fit;

Julius Cæsar, ii, 2, 113: 'that same ague which hath made you lean.'

48. How now? Merely a greeting: 'How d'ye do?'

49. Sweet. Very common as a synonym for 'dear.' Not so saccharine as in modern usage.

50. shrew. Sir Andrew makes an attempt at lively humour.

51. And you too: And God bless you also! Maria uses the regular formula in answering Sir Andrew's 'bless you.' Cf. iii, 1, 76–79; *Hamlet*, iv, 6, 6, 7:

> *Sailor.* God bless you, sir.
> *Horatio.* Let him bless thee too;

King Lear, ii, 1, 1, 2. Wilson oddly enough takes Maria's reply as meaning 'and you're another!'

53. What's that? What does that word *accost* mean? Sir Toby perversely takes 'that' to refer to Maria.

55. chambermaid. Perhaps Sir Toby uses the word in the sense of 'confidential lady-in-waiting' or the like; perhaps he is joking—and mystifying Sir Andrew. The audience, at all events, could not possibly take Maria for a chambermaid in the ordinary sense. She is obviously a 'gentlewoman,' as she is called in i, 5, 173; and, from the outset, she is flirting with Sir Toby, who marries her just before the end of the play (v, 1, 372).

56. I desire better acquaintance. An old formula of politeness: 'I am glad to meet you and hope to know you better in the future.' Cf. *Midsummer Night's Dream*, iii, 1, 185, 186: 'I shall desire you of more acquaintance, good Master Cobweb.'

59. board her. To *board* (French *aborder*) in the sense of 'accost' is common, but the word also suggests the figure of *boarding* a ship.

65, 66. An thou let part so: If you allow her to go without further ceremony.—**never draw sword again:** for such conduct would be unworthy of a knight. Sir Andrew repeats the phrase mechanically, as if it were the proper thing to say.

69. do you think you have fools in hand? Do you think you have fools to deal with? Cf. Marston, *Parasitaster*, iii, 1, 336 (ed. Bullen, II, 172): 'What! did he think he had weak fools in hand?' *Westward Hoe*, iv (Dekker, Pearson ed., II, 332): 'Do you think you haue Fops [i.e., fools] in hand?' Maria's pun is obvious.

71. Marry: sure enough; to be sure; true. *Marry* (originally an oath by the Virgin Mary) is used as a mere interjection. Cf. i, 5, 135; ii, 5, 114; iii, 2, 6.

74. thought is free. A proverb, meaning 'No matter what I may or may not feel at liberty to speak, I can think what I like.' Cf. *Tempest*, iii, 2, 132; Gosson, *The Schoole of Abuse*, 1579, sig. F2 rº: 'Thought is free: you can forbid no man, that vieweth you, to noate you, and that noateth you, to iudge you.'

75. th' butt'ry bar: the bar where drinks are served. The buttery was the storeroom for the *butts* or casks of liquor. Cf. Webster, *The White Devil*, i, 2, 22–24 (ed. Lucas, I, 113): 'If the buttery hatch [i.e., half-door] at Court stood continually open their would be nothing so passionat crouding, nor hot suit after the beverage'; *Look About You*, sc. ix (Hazlitt's Dodsley, VII, 413):

> *Lady Fauconbridge.* Make them drink, Block.
> *Block.* Come to the buttery bar.

77. dry. A dry hand was regarded as an indication of debility. Cf. Chapman, *Monsieur D'Olive*, v (Pearson ed., I, 246), and

Bussy D'Ambois, iii (II, 51). Maria puns on *dry* in the sense of 'thirsty.' Cf. i, 5, 48.

81–83. **a dry jest.** Maria puns on *dry* in the sense of 'sharply witty' and in the literal sense of 'dry,' as applied to Sir Andrew's hand. When he fails to understand her, she dwells on the jest in her next remark. The pun in 'at my fingers' ends' is obvious.

84. **barren:** destitute of all jesting material.

85. **canary.** A favourite sweet wine in Elizabethan times. It came from the Canary Islands.

88–91. **wit:** intelligence.—**a Christian.** Cf. 'even-Christen' in the sense of 'one's fellow creature' (*Hamlet*, v, 1, 32).—**beef.** Sir Andrew's fear accords with the medical science of Shakespeare's time.

100. **the arts:** polite learning. Compare the titles 'Bachelor' and 'Master of Arts.' Sir Toby's pun on *arts* is inevitable, *art* and *nature* being antonyms. But we are not obliged to accept the suggestion that he also puns on *tongues* and *tongs*. For 'curl by' the Folio reads 'coole my.' The emendation is Theobald's.—**bear-baiting.** See iii, 1, 129, note. Sir Andrew's addiction to this sport reminds one of Slender in the *Merry Wives*, i, 1, 298 ff.

102. **mended:** improved.

107. **like flax:** i.e., in long straight strands.—**a distaff:** a staff used in spinning.

113. **she'll none of me:** she'll never accept me.

117, 118. **estate:** rank.—**there's life in't:** your suit promises to be successful. Cf. the proverb 'While there is life there is hope.'

122. **kickshawses:** elegant trifles. The old form of the singular is *kickshaws* (French *quelque chose*, 'something').

124–126. **under the degree of my betters.** Sir Andrew means: 'unless he is of higher rank in society than I am.' He uses a customary phrase of modesty, but in so doing he makes himself doubly ridiculous; for he implies that skill in sports depends, somehow, on social position, and he also seems to say that he's as skilful as anybody who is not more skilful than he!—**I will not compare with an old man.** *Old* is emphatic: 'I do not wish to compare myself with an elderly expert—a veteran.' Another modest disclaimer, expressed in a deliciously absurd fashion.

127. **a galliard.** A very lively and active dance.

130. **the mutton.** In Ford and Dekker, *The Sun's Darling* (Pearson ed., IV, 308), a French dancer is described as 'one that loves mutton so well, he alwaies carries capers about him.'

131. **the back-trick:** a backward step in the galliard, accompanied by an elaborate 'caper' of some kind. Cf. *The Birth of Hercules* (Malone Society ed., ll. 457 ff.): 'We had dauncinge I faith . . .; I neuer see the lyke without minstreles in my lief. They talke of the backe tricke; I faith our Shipp fetcht the backe trick backward and forward to[o].'

134–143. **curtain.** For curtains before portraits see i, 5, 250. —**Are they like:** Are they likely.—**like Mistress Mall's picture:** like a lady's portrait. *Mistress Mall* (i.e., Moll) is merely a general term. No particular Moll is designated. Singer aptly compares the use of 'my lady's' in *Much Ado*, ii, 1, 10.— **coranto:** a rapid-moving dance, as its name ('running') signifies. —**sink-a-pace:** cinque-pace—a kind of galliard.—**virtues:** accomplishments.—**under the star of a galliard.** So Beatrice accounts for her merry heart: 'There was a star danc'd, and under that I was born' (*Much Ado*, ii, 1, 348, 349).

144, 145. **indifferent well:** well enough; pretty well.—**flame-colour'd.** Rowe's emendation for the Folio reading 'dam'd colour'd.' See Textual Notes. Nicholson (*5 Notes and Queries*, X1 [1879], 124) thinks *dam'd colour'd* may mean 'black' or 'dark-coloured,' and Furnivall (*New Shakspere Society Transactions*, 1880–85, Part II, p. 69*) quotes Cotgrave's *Dictionarie*, 1611: 'Couleur d'enfer. . . . Noir-brun enfumé,' and 'Couleur d'enfer. A darke, and smokie browne.'—**stock:** stocking.

146–149. **born under Taurus?** etc. The Twelve Signs of the
Zodiac were supposed to govern or influence different parts of
the body. Old almanacs contain a picture of a man—the *Homo
Signorum*—encircled by the symbols of the Twelve Signs, each
symbol connected by a line with some part of the man's body.
Such a figure was used in determining the time of year when a
particular prescription would be most efficacious. The sign Leo,
not Taurus, governs sides and heart. Taurus, according to some
old authorities, governs neck and throat, but others of equal validity agree with Sir Toby. The treatise entitled *Liber Novem
Iudicum* (cited by Knobel in *Shakespeare's England*, I, 460) as-
signs 'crura et pedes' to Taurus. Richard Whitlock, a seven-
teenth-century physician, says of the quacks of his day that,
when treating a fever, 'if they consult with any rules, it shall be
an *Almanacks*, if the *Moone* say *Purge*, or *Bleed*, the signes of the
Infirmity and its Progresse shall not guide them so much as the
Signes in the *Zodiack*, and that *Antick before Almanacks*, that
beginneth, *Aries Head and Face*, &c. which they have by Heart'
(Ζωοτομία, 1654, p. 49).

Scene IV.

---

5. **his humour** or **my negligence**: capriciousness on his part or
negligent service on mine.—**that**: in that; inasmuch as.

11. **On your attendance, my lord, here**: Here, my lord, await-
ing your orders! *Your* is the objective genitive: 'attending upon
you,' 'at your service.'

12–16. **Stand you aloof.** Addressed to Valentine and all the
rest except Viola.—**no less but all**: no less than everything.—
unclasp'd . . . book. Cf. *1 Henry IV*, i, 3, 188: 'And now I will
unclasp a secret book.'—**address thy gait**: direct thy steps.—
accéss. Note the accent.

22. unprofited: unsuccessful.

25. Surprise her: overpower her; break down her defences. Cf. *Timon*, v, 1, 158, 159: 'You . . . Surprise me to the very brink of tears.'—**dear:** heartfelt. *Dear* is often used to emphasize the meaning of a noun. Cf. v, 1, 74.

28. Than . . . aspéct: than she would in the acting of a messenger of more dignified appearance.

32–34. rubious: ruby-red.—**shrill and sound:** high in pitch and clear; not cracked. Cf. *Hamlet*, ii, 2, 446.—**And all . . . part:** and everything about thee well befits a woman's part in a play.

35. thy constellation: thy appearance, character, and disposition; thy nature (as determined by the stars that ruled at the time of thy birth).—**apt:** fit.

41. a barful strife! Alas, an effort that it is much against my will to undertake! Literally, 'full of bars'—i.e., 'impediments.' Wilson follows Daniel in reading 'ah! barful strife!' But emphasis on *ah* destroys the metre.

Scene V.

2. as: that.

6. fear no colours. An old proverbial phrase for 'fear nothing.' Cf. *2 Henry IV*, v, 5, 90–94:

> *Falstaff.* This that you heard was but a colour [i.e., a pretext].
> *Shallow.* A colour that I fear you will die in, Sir John.
> *Falstaff.* Fear no colours!

The phrase was used (like many such colloquial tags) with no thought of its derivation or literal meaning. Probably *no colours* originally signified 'no flags,' as Maria's interpretation suggests. The Clown puns on *collar*, 'the hangman's noose.'

9. lenten: lean—good enough, no doubt, for lent, but showing no great abundance of wit. Cf. 'lenten entertainment' in the sense of 'a poor reception' (*Hamlet*, ii, 2, 329).

12, 13. that . . . foolery: you may confidently use that answer to the conundrum in your jesting talk.

15, 16. God . . . have it . . . talents: May God enable those who (like you) have the full possession of their wits to use their wits wisely; and let fools make what use they can of their small stock of intellect. Feste suggests that he must rely on his skill as a jester to induce his mistress to overlook his truancy. The dialogue in ll. 40 ff. shows that his confidence is not misplaced. *Talents* or *tallants* is a common form of *talons*, and doubtless Feste is punning on that word: 'Let them use their own claws (their natural weapons) to defend themselves.' Cf. Gosson, *The Schoole of Abuse*, 1579 (Shakespeare Society ed., p. 32): 'God hath armed every creature against his enemie: the lyon with pawes, the bull with hornes, the bore with tuskes, the vulture with tallents.' Halliwell cites *Love's Labour's Lost* (iv, 2, 65, 66) for a pun on *talent* and *talon*.

22. for: as for.—**bear it out:** make it endurable.

25, 26. if one break. Maria puns on *points*—tagged laces that attached the breeches to the doublet (jacket).—**gaskins:** galligaskins, loose breeches.

27. Apt: to the point; clever.

30, 31. thou wert . . . Eve's flesh: you would make as clever a wife for him.

33. you were best: it would be best for you. Cf. ii, 2, 27; iii, 4, 11, 12.

37. wits: sane and clever persons.

39. Quinapalus. Feste invents the name of the philosopher he pretends to quote. Cf. ii, 3, 22, 23.

45. Go to. A phrase of rejection or contempt. It means, literally, 'go away!' like our colloquial 'go way' (which is an old idiom). It may be used in expostulation, reproof, impatience, or incredulity. Sometimes it merely closes or shuts off discourse, like 'very well!' or 'enough said!' Cf. ii, 5, 164; iii, 4, 57, 105; iv, 1, 3.—**dry:** stupid. Cf. i, 3, 75–77.

46. **you grow dishonest:** you are becoming untrustworthy. *Dishonest* is a vague term for any infraction of honourable principles or conduct. Here Olivia applies it to the fault for which Maria has just threatened Feste with punishment: that is, playing truant—'being so long absent' (l. 17).

47–59. **madonna:** my lady.—**dry:** thirsty.—**mend himself:** reform.—**botcher.** The regular old term for a tailor who mends clothing.—**Anything . . . virtue,** etc. Feste parodies the formal style of the logicians. He undertakes to prove that no human being is either all bad or all good.—**will serve:** will answer—i.e., will satisfy you as an excuse for my fault.—**so:** well and good!— **what remedy?** There's no help for it—I must submit to misfortune. Then Feste solemnly adds two maxims—one original, the other trite. Taken together, they remind Olivia that, as every man must yield to the inevitable, so must every woman, for beauty is a flower that fades.—**there is no true cuckold but calamity:** Every man is wedded to fortune; hence, when one's fortune is unfaithful, one may in very truth be called a cuckold— the husband of an unfaithful wife.—**The lady . . . away.** Feste turns aside from Olivia and addresses Malvolio.

61–64. **Misprision in the highest degree!** An error of the worst kind! You meant *me*, but should have meant *yourself*; for *you* are the fool, not *I*.—**cucullus non facit monachum:** A cowl doesn't make a monk. So, Feste argues, his motley (particoloured) uniform does not prove him a fool. For the proverb see *Measure for Measure*, v, 1, 263; Apperson, *English Proverbs*, p. 308. Cf. Whetstone, *Promos*, iii, 6: 'A holie Hoode, makes not a Frier deuoute.'—**to prove you a fool.** Cf. *King Lear*, i, 4, 106 ff.

66. **Dexteriously.** An old by-form of *dexterously*—not a verbal trick of Feste's.

68, 69. **Good my mouse of virtue:** My good little virtuous mouse. *Mouse* was often used as a term of playful affection. Craig (in Luce's edition) quotes Nicholas Breton, *Miseries of Mavillia* (ed. Grosart, II, 37): 'My father would . . . call mee good gyrle, sweete mouse, owne wenche and dads byrd.' Cf. *Hamlet*, iii, 4, 183; *Love's Labour's Lost*, v, 2, 19. For the position of *good* compare 'Good my lord' (v, 1, 109).

70, 71. **idleness:** trivial occupation to pass away the time.—**I'll bide your proof:** I'll wait patiently for you to prove your statement.

80. **mend:** improve.

81. **Yes.** Malvolio, who does not enjoy Feste's jesting talk, means that he grows more and more foolish the longer he lives.

89–95. **barren:** stupid.—**with:** by.—**out of his guard:** defenceless.—**minister occasion:** afford opportunity.—**crow:** i.e., with laughter. Cf. *As You Like It*, ii, 7, 30–33:

> My lungs began to crow like chanticleer
> That fools should be so deep contemplative;
> And I did laugh sans intermission
> An hour by his dial;

Two Gentlemen, ii, 1, 27, 28: 'You were wont, when you laughed, to crow like a cock.'—**these set kind of fools:** fools of this artificial sort.—**zanies:** subordinate buffoons who attend upon professional jesters, imitate them, and serve as butts for their jokes.

96–99. **of:** because of; with.—**distemper'd:** diseased, unhealthy. Cf. ii, 1, 4.—**generous:** high-minded.—**birdbolts:** blunt arrows used for shooting birds.—**an allow'd fool:** a privileged fool—one who has, as it were, a license to practise his profession. Cf. *King Lear*, i, 4, 220: 'your all-licens'd fool.'

105, 106. **Now Mercury . . . fools!** Now may Mercury endow thee with the art of lying! Mercury was the god of craftiness and trickery. His help, Feste suggests, will be necessary if Olivia is to continue her defence of fools and foolery.

119. **old:** outworn, trite.

121–123. **should be:** were destined to be.—**Jove.** See ii, 5, 190, note.—**pia mater:** brain—literally, the inner membrane enclosing the brain. Cf. Nashe, *Strange Newes*, 1593 (ed. Grosart, II, 272): 'Thou turmoilst thy *pia mater* to proue base births better than the offspring of many discents.'

129, 130. **A plague o' these pickle-herring!** Sir Toby's announcement has been followed by a hiccough, which he apologetically ascribes to herring rather than to drink.—**How now, sot?** How d'ye do, fool! *Sot* is not here used in the sense of 'drunkard.' Cf. v, 1, 202.

131. **Cousin:** uncle. See i, 3, 5, note.

135. **Ay, marry:** Yes, to be sure. See i, 3, 71, note.

137. **faith:** to enable me to resist the devil. So in *The Comedy of Errors*, iii, 2, 150, 151, Dromio declares that the fact that his 'breast was made of faith' had saved him from witchcraft.—**it's all one:** no matter about that! Cf. v, 1, 201, 380, 416.

140. **above heat:** 'above the state of being warm in a proper degree' (Steevens). Cf. *Merchant of Venice*, i, 1, 79–82:

> Let me play the fool.
> With mirth and laughter let old wrinkles come,
> And let my liver rather heat with wine
> Than my heart cool with mortifying groans.

142. **crowner:** coroner.—**sit o':** hold an inquest on.

148. **takes on him:** takes upon himself; presumes.

156, 157. **Has:** he has.—**a sheriff's post.** 'The houses of mayors and sheriffs of towns were distinguished by large posts set up before the doors. These posts were often elaborately carved' (Halliwell).

160. **Why, of mankind:** Why, just like the general run of human beings.

166–172. **a squash:** an unripe peascod (pea pod).—**codling:** an unripe apple—what we call a 'green apple.'—**in standing**

water: like the tide in the interval between ebb and flood, when it moves neither way.—**well-favour'd:** handsome. *Favour* is common in the sense of one's 'features.'—**One would think ... him:** To judge by his fretful tone and manner, one would think him only just weaned. The expression was proverbial. Cf. George Wilkins, *The Miseries of Inforst Marriage*, 1607, sig. F3, lf. 1 v°: 'Their mothers milke not wrung out of their nose yet.' See Tilley, *Philological Quarterly*, VI (1927), 307, 308.

173. **my gentlewoman:** my lady-in-waiting. See i, 3, 55, note.

187, 188. **con:** study, learn.—**let me sustain no scorn:** do not subject me to any scornful treatment.—**comptible:** sensitive.— **sinister:** uncivil.

191. **modest:** moderate, reasonable.

194. **comedian.** In the general sense of 'actor.'

195, 196. **my profound heart:** my excellent deep-thinking lady. *Heart* (or *hearts*) is often used as a vocative in familiar or lightly affectionate address. Cf. ii, 3, 16. By *profound* Viola suggests, in a jesting vein, that it was a 'deep thought' to infer that she is a comedian. Of course she knows that Olivia's question was not meant seriously.—**and yet ... play:** and yet I challenge my bitterest enemy to deny that I am playing a part. This remark is understood by the audience but not by Olivia.

198. **If I do not usurp myself:** if I am not in wrongful possession of my own personality; if I am really what I am.

199–201. **you do usurp yourself; ... reserve.** Viola catches up Olivia's word *usurp* and applies it in a different sense: 'You *do* make a wrong use of yourself; for it is your duty as a woman to give yourself to a husband.'—**this is from my commission:** this is not the message with which I am entrusted. Cf. l. 191: 'out of my part.' *From* is emphatic: 'away from,' 'foreign to' (cf. v, 1, 340). Viola pretends that she has committed her message to memory and that all this talk interrupts its delivery. —**I will on:** I will proceed.

204. **forgive you:** excuse you from repeating.

214, 215. **'Tis not that time of moon ... dialogue:** I am not just now so subject to the moon's influence as to take part in such a fantastic dialogue. Olivia alludes to the moon's supposed influence in causing lunacy. *Skipping* suggests also the inconstancy of which the ever-changing moon is a symbol. Olivia implies that Viola's talk is not quite coherent.

216. **Here lies your way.** With a gesture of dismissal. Tilley (*Philological Quarterly*, VI [1927], 309) notes the fuller form in *Heywood's Proverbs*, 1562 (Spenser Society ed., p. 29): 'Here is the doore, and there is the wey.' Cf. *Taming of the Shrew*, iii, 2, 212: 'The door is open, sir; there lies your way.'

217. **swabber.** A petty officer whose duty was 'to make and keep the ship clean, and that as well in the great cabin as everywhere betwixt the decks' (Capt. Nathaniel Boteler, *A Dialogicall Discourse concerninge Marine Affaires*, 1634, ed. Perrin, p. 11). Cf. *Tempest*, ii, 2, 48, 49: 'The master, the swabber, the boatswain, and I, The gunner, and his mate.'—**to hull:** to lie adrift with all sails furled. Cf. *Richard III*, iv, 4, 433–439:

> On the western coast
> Rideth a puissant navy; . . .
> . . . .
> And there they hull, expecting but the aid
> Of Buckingham to welcome them ashore;

Henry VIII, ii, 4, 199, 200: 'hulling in The wild sea of my conscience'; Massinger, *A Very Woman*, v, 5 (Gifford, 2d ed., IV, 343): 'We were becalm'd, and hull'd so up and down twelve hours.' For the nautical term *hull*, *lie at hull*, or *lie a-hull* see Albert Matthews, *New-England Historical and Genealogical Register*, April, 1905.

218. **Some mollification for your giant:** 'Ladies, in romance, are guarded by giants, who repel all improper or troublesome advances. Viola, seeing [Maria] so eager to oppose her message,

intreats Olivia to pacify her giant' (Johnson). Cf. ii, 5, 15 ('the
little villain'); iii, 2, 71 ('the youngest wren of nine').

221, 222. **deliver:** report.—**when the courtesy of it is so fearful:** when, instead of polite manners, you assume so defiant an
air. Olivia jestingly refers to the obstinate insistence that Viola
has shown (as reported by Malvolio in ll. 147 ff.).—**your office:**
the errand with which you are charged; your business.

225–227. **overture:** declaration.—**no taxation of homage:** no
demand for surrender and submission.—**the olive.** The symbol
of peace.—**matter:** subject matter, substance.

232–234. **my entertainment:** the manner in which I have been
received.—**maidenhead:** maidenhood.—**divinity:** sacred discourse.—**profanation:** the impious disclosure of a sacred message.

245. **by the method:** in accordance with the preaching style
that you have adopted.

249–254. **out of your text:** for you are now speaking of *faces*,
not of *hearts*.—**such ... present:** This is the kind of person I was
just a moment ago—i.e., this is the picture that you wished to
see. *This present* is adverbial—'just now.'

255. **if God did all.** The Elizabethan dramatists never tire of
satirical remarks about artificial aids to beauty.

256. **in grain:** dyed in fast colours. *Grain* is the regular word
for the red dye derived from the *coccus* insect (cochineal), which,
when dried, looks like a kind of grain. Cf. *Comedy of Errors*, iii,
2, 108, 109.

258–261. **cunning:** skilful.—**she.** Often used as a noun.—
graces: beauties.—**no copy.** Compare the theme of *Sonnets*
i–xiv; *Romeo and Juliet*, i, 1, 222–227. In the speech that follows
Olivia refuses to take Viola's words in the sense intended and
interprets *copy* literally.

264–268. **utensil:** a furnishing—a detail which helps to furnish me with the beauty you speak of.—**labell'd to my will:** entered in a slip of parchment attached to my last will and testa-

ment.—**item:** literally, 'also.' Used originally with all the articles in a list or inventory except the first (as in *Two Gentlemen*, iii, 1, 302 ff.), but often (as here) applied to all of them. Cf. *1 Henry IV*, ii, 4, 584 ff.—**indifferent:** more or less; rather (cf. i, 3, 144).—**to praise me:** to appraise me; to make an inventory of my qualities. Olivia is manifestly punning on the other sense of *praise*.

270. **if:** even if.—**the devil:** whose pride is supreme in degree. Compare the proverbial phrase 'as proud as Lucifer.'

274. **with.** Omitted in the Folio; supplied by Pope.—**fertile:** plenteous, abundant.

279–281. **In voices well divulg'd, free,** etc.: well reputed by public testimony as of noble nature, etc.—**free.** Cf. *Othello*, iii, 3, 199: 'your free and noble nature.'—**dimension.** Synonymous with *the shape of nature* (i.e., his natural form). Cf. v, 1, 244. This phrase is added as an explanation of *dimension*. *And* is the so-called 'epexegetical (explanatory) *and*'—a very common idiomatic use of that conjunction.—**gracious:** full of grace—i.e., of beauty.

284. **such . . . life:** with such intensity that his life is merely one long pang of death. *Suffering* is (like *deadly*) an adjective modifying *life*.

287–292. **a willow cabin:** a tent of willow boughs. The weeping willow was the symbol of disconsolate love. Cf. *Hamlet*, iv, 7, 168; *Othello*, iv, 3, 42 ff.—**my soul:** i.e., you, Olivia.—**cantons:** songs.—**reverberate:** reverberating, reëchoing.—**the babbling gossip of the air:** echo.

295. **But:** but that.

297. **my state:** my condition in life. Cf. i, 2, 44.

303. **fee'd post:** hired messenger.

305–307. **that.** The antecedent is implied in *his* (= *of him*).—**Plac'd in contempt:** held in contempt; despised.—**cruelty.** Cf. ii, 4, 83.

310. **thou art.** Olivia, in conversing with Viola, has used the formal pronoun *you*. Now, in soliloquy (that is, to all intents and purposes, in thought), she changes to the familiar and affectionate *thou*.

312, 313. **blazon:** heraldic warrant of gentility. *Blazon* is, literally, the description of a coat of arms in the proper heraldic terms.—**soft!** slowly! Used as an interjection to warn against haste.—**Unless the master were the man.** Olivia implies that she might well accept Orsino if he were as irresistibly attractive as this servant of his.

315. **perfections.** Cf. i, 1, 39.

317. **To creep in at mine eyes:** and thus take possession of my mind and heart.—**let it be!** Thus Olivia yields to fate. Cf. ll. 329, 330.

319. **peevish:** childishly ill-tempered. Olivia is thinking of Viola's parting words (ll. 303–307).

320–322. **County's:** Count's. *Count* in this play is loosely used as a synonym for *Duke*.—**I'll none of it:** I'll have nothing to do with it; I've no use for it. A common old idiom of rejection. Cf. ii, 2, 8.—**to flatter with his lord:** to give his master any false encouragement.

324. **If that:** if. See i, 2, 48, note.

327, 328. **to find . . . mind:** to find that my eye, which has been so attracted by this young man, may induce me to yield to a passion which my judgment cannot approve.

329, 330. **Ourselves we do not owe:** We mortals do not own ourselves; we are not our own masters but the slaves of destiny. —**decreed:** i.e., by fate; fated. Cf. *Romeo and Juliet*, iv, 1, 21, note; Apperson, *English Proverbs*, p. 560.

Act II. Scene I.

1. nor . . . not. Such double negatives are common. The doubling emphasizes the negation, as in Anglo-Saxon and Greek. Cf. iii, 1, 171.

3–8. By your patience. A courteous formula: 'by your kind permission'; 'if you will agree with me in my wishes.'—**malignancy:** bad astrological influence. The word suggests also the medical sense.—**distemper:** infect.—**evils:** misfortunes.

11–17. sooth: in very truth; truly.—**My . . . extravagancy:** The course of travel upon which I have decided is out-and-out vagrancy; I have no definite plan. Cf. *Othello*, i, 1, 137, 138: 'an extravagant and wheeling stranger Of here and everywhere.'— **But.** Sebastian changes his mind in a moment and confides in Antonio.—**touch:** feeling. Wright compares *Midsummer Night's Dream*, iii, 2, 285, 286: 'Have you no modesty, no maiden shame, No touch of bashfulness?'—**it charges me,** etc.: I feel under some obligation—as a point of good manners— to tell you who I am and what my purposes are.—**Messaline.** There is no such town. Hanmer reads *Metelin*. Capell conjectures 'Mitylene.'

21–24. in an hour: in one and the same hour.—**some hour:** about an hour.—**the breach:** the breaking waves.

28–31. with such estimable wonder: with so much admiration in my estimate of her.—**that.** Emphatic.—**envy.** Emphatic: 'even *malice*.' *Envy* is common in this general sense.— **She is drown'd,** etc. Cf. *Hamlet*, iv, 7, 187, 188: 'Too much of water hast thou, poor Ophelia, And therefore I forbid my tears' (Steevens).

34. your bad entertainment: the poorness of the rough hospitality that I have afforded you.

36. murther me: i.e., by forcing me to part company with you.—**for:** in return for.

39–43. recover'd: rescued.—**the manners of my mother:** my mother's temperament. Malone compares *Henry V*, iv, 6, 28–32:

> The pretty and sweet manner of it forc'd
> Those waters from me which I would have stopp'd;
> But I had not so much of man in me,
> And all my mother came into mine eyes
> And gave me up to tears.

—**tell tales of me:** reveal how unmanly I am. The convention that 'tears are womanish' (*Romeo and Juliet*, iii, 3, 110) occurs in great variety of expression. See *As You Like It*, iii, 4, 3; *King John*, iv, 1, 35, 36; *Richard III*, i, 2, 164; *Coriolanus*, v, 6, 45; *Macbeth*, iv, 2, 28, 29; iv, 3, 230; *King Lear*, i, 4, 318–326; ii, 4, 280, 281; *Antony and Cleopatra*, iv, 2, 34–36.

45. gentleness: love and favour.

Scene II.

This scene takes place in the street and at a short distance from Olivia's mansion. 'At several doors' in the stage direction means 'each at one of the two doors at the back of the stage.' Only time enough has elapsed since Malvolio's exit at the end of Act I to allow for the first scene of Act II.

6–12. to have taken: by taking.—**a desperate assurance:** a certainty that leaves him no hope of any change of mind on her part.—**will none of him.** Cf. i, 5, 321.—**to come:** as to come.—**in his affairs:** on his business.—**your lord's taking of this:** that your lord has accepted this message of rejection and will trouble her no more.—**Receive it so:** Take the ring back on these terms —with this understanding.

13. She took the ring of me. Viola (who has not failed to understand Olivia's words and manner in their recent interview) perceives that this ring is a love token from Olivia. But she must not reveal the facts of the case to Malvolio; and so she falls in with Olivia's fiction—that the ring had been sent by the Duke.

19. not. This repeats and emphasizes the negative idea of *forbid*. Cf. ii, 1, 1.

21. her eyes had lost her tongue: the intensity of her gaze had deprived her of the power of coherent speech. *Lost* is causative: 'made her lose.'

23, 24. cunning: craftiness.—**in:** in the person of.

26. I am the man: the man of her choice. Cf. *As You Like It*, iii, 3, 2, 3: 'And how, Audrey, am I the man yet?'

27. she were better. In the idiom *you were better*, *you* was originally a dative. It was felt as a nominative, however, and '*I* (*thou, he, she*) were better' was used instead of *me* (*thee, him, her*). Cf. i, 5, 33; iii, 4, 11, 12.

28, 29. Disguise ... much: Since disguise is a form of deceit, the father of lies, the devil—that artful enemy of mankind— takes advantage of my using such trickery to carry out plans of his own.

30. the proper false: men who are handsome but deceitful.

33. such as we are made of, such we be: we are composed of frail material, and therefore we are frail.

34, 35. How will this fadge? How will this fit? How can this state of things adjust itself to any reasonable outcome? For everything seems to be at cross purposes.—**monster:** because both man and woman.—**fond:** dote.

38. My state is desperate for my master's love: I cannot hope to win my master's love, since he does not know I am a woman. —**state:** condition. Cf. v, 1, 67.

40. thriftless: unprofitable, unavailing.

Scene III.

1–9. **Not . . . betimes,** etc. The Elizabethans amused themselves and sharpened their wits by devising paradoxes and arguing logically to prove them. Sir Toby plays this game. His demonstration (in ll. 6–9) depends on the ambiguity of 'early'; for late at night may be early in the morning. Sir Andrew is too stupid to follow the whimsical argument.

2–4. **betimes:** in good season.—**diluculo surgere.** An old maxim once familiar to every schoolboy, from Lily's Latin Grammar: 'Diluculo surgere saluberrimum est'—'to rise at dawn is very good for the health.' Sir Andrew understands it well enough, but he fails to see how the quotation confirms Sir Toby's remark—as, indeed, it does not!—**by my troth.** An oath by one's plighted (pledged) faith. Cf. i, 3, 3.

9, 10. **Does not . . . elements?** According to ancient science, every living creature owes life and health to the harmonious blend of the four elements (fire, air, earth, and water) in his system. Cf. *Henry V*, iii, 7, 22–24; *Antony and Cleopatra*, v, 2, 292–293. The doctrine is too abstruse for Sir Andrew, whose observation has convinced him that human life is maintained by food and drink. Thus, without knowing it, he anticipates science's repudiation of the ancient doctrine.

13, 14. **Th'art a scholar!** You are right! You have the correct theory of life! I accept your doctrine, and we will follow it in practice. Let us eat and drink.—**stoup:** a large cup or goblet. Cf. l. 129.

16, 17. **my hearts:** my fine fellows. Often used, commonly in the vocative, as a term of friendship or *camaraderie*. Cf. i, 5, 195; *Tempest*, i, 1, 5: 'Heigh, my hearts! Cheerly, cheerly, my hearts!'—**the picture of We Three?** A picture (sometimes an inn sign) of two idiotic heads—the person who looks at it being of

course the third fool. Apparently the picture was sometimes
furnished with a motto: 'We three loggerheads be.' Cf. Phineas
Fletcher, *The Purple Island*, viii, 54:

> Upon his shield two laughing fools you see,
> (In number he the third, first in degree)
> At which himself would laugh, and fleer: his word, *We three*.

18. **a catch:** a round. See l. 61, note.

19–29. **breast:** voice. *Breath* in l. 21 is a synonym. Cf. John
Heywood, *The Spider and the Flie*, 1556 (Spenser Society ed.,
p. 27). 'As breath and breast wolde beare, loudely he cryde.'—
gracious: pleasing, delightful.—**Pigrogromitus . . . Queubus.**
Mere high-sounding nonsense—the kind of fooling that jesters
practised when true wit and humour were not needed. It suits
Sir Andrew to a T. Cf. i, 5, 39.—**leman:** sweetheart.—**I did
impeticos thy gratillity:** I pocketed your little gratuity.—**impeticos:** literally, put it in my petticoat—i.e., the pocket of my
gown. We need not 'correct' it to *impeticoat*, as some editors do,
though it may be a misprint. *Gratillity* is manifestly a diminutive; but we are not to suppose that Sir Andrew takes it in that
sense.—**for Malvolio's nose . . . bottle-ale houses.** Pure nonsense
again—to please Sir Andrew. The efforts of some critics to extort
a meaning are wasted energy.—**the Myrmidons:** the troop of
Achilles. See *Troilus and Cressida*, v, 7, 1 ff.

30, 31. **when all is done:** after all—a phrase emphasizing the
superlative.

35. **testril:** a tester; a sixpence. The word appears to be a
diminutive—like Feste's 'gratillity.' Doubtless Sir Andrew is
under the spell of Feste's word and echoes it without perceiving
that *testril* would mean 'a little sixpence.'—**of:** from.

36. **a song of good life:** a song that teaches one how to live
righteously; a moral ditty. Feste's question is deliberately comic
under the circumstances. Sir Andrew's reply, in which he

declares his addiction to what we call a 'fast' life, is uninten-
tionally comic. His physique is hardly that of a typical sport!

44. **in lovers meeting**: when lovers meet. *Meeting* is not a
noun but a participle agreeing with *lovers*.

50–52. **still**: always.—**sweet and twenty**! sweet, and twenty
times sweet! sweet in the twentieth degree! Steevens compares
The Wit of a Woman, 1604, sig. D2 vᵒ: 'Sweet and twenty, all
sweet and sweet.'

56, 57. **contagious breath**: a 'catchy' voice—with a pun on
breath and on *contagious*. Sir Andrew does not understand the
coarse jest, and Sir Toby explains (to the audience), and then
changes the subject with 'But.'

58–61. **To hear by the nose . . . contagion:** If we may use our
noses for hearing as well as for smelling, we may say that the
Fool's breath is sweet to hear but malodorous.—**make the welkin
dance**: sing a song that shall be loud and merry enough to make
the stars in the sky dance to our tune. Cf. *Much Ado*, ii, 1, 349:
'there was a star danc'd'; *Coriolanus*, v, 4, 52–54:

> The trumpets, sackbuts, psalteries, and fifes,
> Tabors and cymbals and the shouting Romans
> Make the sun dance.

Dr. Johnson interprets: 'drink till the sky seems to turn round.'
But Sir Toby is speaking of singing, not of drinking.—**draw three
souls out of one weaver?** Weavers were noted for singing. Cf. *1
Henry IV*, ii, 4, 147, 148: 'I would I were a weaver; I could sing
psalms or anything.' 'Our song,' Sir Toby means, 'will be so
melodious as to enchant the soul of a weaver and draw it out of
his body to listen: nay, it will be good enough to draw three
souls out of one weaver (and that will certainly be a miracle).'
Warburton compares *Much Ado*, ii, 3, 60–62. 'Now is his soul
ravish'd! Is it not strange that sheep's guts should hale souls out
of men's bodies?'

63. **An:** if.—**I am dog:** I am very skilful; I'm a regular adept. Halliwell cites Haughton, *Englishmen for My Money*, ed. 1616, sig. A3, lf. 2 v°: 'I remember my great Grandfathers Grandmothers sisters coosen told mee, that Pigges and *French-men*, speake one Language, *awee, awee*; I am Doggee at this.' Cf. *Two Gentlemen*, iv, 4, 14, 15: 'to be, as it were, a dog at all things.'; Dekker, *Worke for Armorours*, 1609 (ed. Grosart, IV, 162): 'A lane of Brokers, who handled their Pieces passing well, & were old dog at a marke.'

65. **By'r Lady.** Originally an oath by 'our Lady'—the Virgin Mary.

66. **'Thou knave.'** The words of this catch are 'Hold thy peace, thou knave; and I prithee hold thy peace.' In singing, the three parts are so arranged that each of the three singers is called 'thou knave.' See Furness's *New Variorum*, p. 118.

71. **'Tis not the first time I have constrained one.** Sir Andrew means that he has often shown his valour by provoking a quarrel.

76. **caterwauling.** Cf. *Titus Andronicus*, iv, 2, 57: 'Why, what a caterwauling dost thou keep!'

80–84. **a Catayan:** a native of Cathay (China). It was a slang term for a 'cheat,' a 'humbug.' Cf. *Merry Wives*, ii, 1, 148–150: 'I will not believe such a Cataian, though the priest o' th' town commended him for a true man.' Sir Toby uses the word as a mere term of contempt: 'What do I care for your lady?'—**politicians:** statesmen. 'We are occupied with an important matter of statesmanship.'—**a Peg-a-Ramsey.** Peg of Ramsey or Peggie Ramsey is the sportive heroine of an old song and dance tune (see Chappell, *Popular Music of the Olden Time*, p. 218). Sir Toby merely expresses extreme contempt: 'Malvolio's a light-headed fellow of no account.' This makes a good comic introduction for Malvolio, who enters at l. 93 with his usual air of solemn propriety.—**'Three merry men be we.'** An old song. Steevens cites Peele, *The Old Wive's Tale*, ll. 20 ff. (ed. Bullen, I, 304):

'Let us rehearse the old proverb—Three merry men, and three
merry men, And three merry men be we; I in the wood, and
thou on the ground, And Jack sleeps in the tree.' For the tune
see Naylor, *Shakespeare and Music*, 1896, p. 189.

84, 85. **consanguineous:** or, as Sir Toby translates—'of her
blood.'—**Tilly-vally.** An interjection of contempt: 'fiddle-
faddle'; 'fiddlesticks.' 'Don't talk to me about "my lady"! I am
just as good as she is!' Cf. *2 Henry IV*, ii, 4, 90: 'Tilly-fally, Sir
John, ne'er tell me!'; Skelton, Riverside ed., I, 35: 'Tully vally,
strawe, let be, I say!' Then Sir Toby sings a bit of the old song
on the story of Susanna and the Elders: 'The Constancy of
Susanna' (*Roxburghe Ballads*, ed. Chappell, I, 190–193):

> There dwelt a man in Babylon,
>   of reputation great by fame;
> He took to wife a faire woman,
>   Susanna she was called by name;
> A woman faire and vertuous:
>   Lady, lady,
> Why should wee not of her learne thus
>   to liue godly?

86. **Beshrew:** literally, 'curse'; but regularly used in a light
sense.

87–90. **dispos'd:** inclined to make merry. Cf. *Love's Labour's
Lost*, v, 2, 466: 'To make my lady laugh when she's dispos'd.'—
natural: naturally. Thus Sir Andrew, in effect, calls himself a
natural—i.e., a born fool, an idiot. Cf. i, 3, 30.

91. **O' . . . December.** The old ballad of *Musselburgh Field*
(Child, No. 172, III, 378) begins:

> On the tenth day of December,
>   And the fourth yeere of King Edwards raigne,
> Att Musleboorrowe, as I remember,
>   Two goodly hosts there mett on a plaine.

Cf. Brome, *The Court Beggar*, iv, 3 (Pearson ed., I, 246, 247):

> *Ferdinand.* The Battaile of Musleborough Field was a brave one.
> *Frederick.* O do you fly out agen?
> *Ferd.* *Sings part of the old Song, and acts it madly.*

—twelf. An old form of *twelfth.* The Folio uses it in the title of the play: 'Twelfe Night.'

93–99. My masters: Gentlemen.—**wit:** common sense.—**honesty:** regard for honourable conduct; decency.—**tinkers:** proverbially given to talkative drunkenness.—**coziers':** cobblers'.—**catches.** Cf. l. 18.—**mitigation or remorse.** Synonymous: 'softening.' Malvolio affects a dignified and elegant style. *Remorse* is often used for 'compassion.'—**respect of:** consideration for.

101. Sneck up! Be hanged! Cf. Dekker, *The Shoemaker's Holiday* (Pearson ed., I, 18): 'let him goe snicke-vp'; Middleton, *Blurt, Master Constable*, iv, 1, 50, 51 (ed. Bullen, I, 72): 'And [i.e., if] you will not believe me, marry, foh! I have been believed of your betters, marry, snick up!'

102–104. round: outspoken.—**disorders:** disorderly conduct.

110. 'Farewell . . . be gone.' The beginning of the old song 'Corydon's Farewell to Phyllis.' The first two stanzas are as follows:

> Farewell, dear love, since thou wilt needs be gon,
> Mine eies do shew my life is almost done;
> Nay, I will never die, so long as I can spie,
> There be many mo, though that she do go
> There be many mo, I feare not,
> Why, then, let her goe, I care not.

> Farewell, farewell, since this I finde is true,
> I will not spend more time in wooing you;
> But I will seeke elsewhere, if I may find her there.
> Shall I bid her goe? What, and if I doe?
> Shall I bid her go and spare not?
> Oh, no, no, no, no, I dare not.

See Halliwell, *Outlines*, 2d ed., 1882, pp. 264, 265; Robert Jones, *First Booke of Songes and Ayres*, 1600 (ed. Fellowes, 1925, pp. 24, 25); Percy, *Reliques*, 1765, I, 187–189.

111–114. **Nay.** Merely a term of expostulation. 'Is't even so?' is likewise expostulatory: 'Is *this* the kind of conduct we have to put up with?'

116. **there you lie.** In modern stage business Sir Toby is made to fall flat on the floor. We may well doubt if that was Shakespeare's intention. 'There you lie' gives excellent sense without any such buffoonery: 'In *that* point, at all events, you're a liar! for you certainly are not immortal.'

119. **an if:** if.

120. **spare not?** refrain not? not shrink from so decisive an action?

125. **cakes and ale.** Cf. Nashe, *Pasquil's Returne*, 1589 (ed. McKerrow, I, 71): 'They are ready to greete you with a Cake and a cup of Ale in euery Parrish.'

126. **ginger.** A favourite spice for ale in old times. It was thought to reduce the intoxicating effect. Cf. *Histriomastix*, i (ed. Simpson, II, 21):

> Ale gives a buffet in the head,
> But ginger under-proppes the brayne;

Lodge and Greene, *A Looking Glasse for London and England*, 1594 (ed. Grosart, XIV, 44): 'All Niniuie hath not such a cup of Ale . . .; by my troth, I spent eleuen pence, besides three rases [i.e., roots] of ginger.'

128. **your chain.** Malvolio wears a gold chain as a sign of his office as steward of the household. Cf. ii, 5, 66.

130–133. **priz'd:** appraised, valued.—**give means.** Malvolio refers to Sir Toby's calling on Maria for 'a stoup of wine' (l. 129). —**uncivil rule:** disorderly (riotous) behaviour. Cf. Gascoigne, *Supposes*, iii, 1 (ed. Bond, *Early Plays from the Italian*, p. 38):

'What noise, what a rule is this?' Copland, *The Hye Way to the Spyttel House*, l. 255 (ed. Hazlitt, *Early Popular Poetry*, IV, 36): 'This rule make they euery day and nyght'; Heywood, *The English Traveller*, i, 2 (Pearson ed., IV, 16):

> Prying
> To see what dainty fare our kitchin yeelds,
> What Guests we harbour, and what rule we keepe;

Midsummer Night's Dream, iii, 2, 5: 'What night-rule now about this haunted grove?'—**by this hand.** A common oath.

134. **Go shake your ears!** like the ass that you are. A stock phrase of contemptuous dismissal. Cf. *Julius Cæsar*, iv, 1, 25–27.

> Then take we down his load, and turn him off
> (Like to the empty ass) to shake his ears
> And graze in commons;

Roxburghe Ballads, ed. Chappell, II, 555: 'And Tom may go shake his long eares like an asse' (with a picture of Tom with ass's ears); *The Conflict of Conscience*, ii, 3 (1581, sig. Cij v°): 'For nether of you both, a pin doo I care: Goe shake your eares both.'

135–136. **as good a deed as to drink.** An old humorous comparison. Cf. *1 Henry IV*, ii, 2, 25–27: 'An 'twere not as good a deed as drink to turn true man and to leave these rogues, I am the veriest varlet that ever chewed with a tooth.' Sir Andrew's comical confusion of hunger with thirst reminds one of his philosophical observation in ll. 11, 12.—**to challenge him the field:** to call him to the field (of battle) by a challenge.

141–147. **Sweet.** Not so saccharine an adjective as now-a-days. It is common as a mere synonym for *dear*. Cf. i, 3, 49. —**be patient:** be calm; control yourself.—**For:** as for.—**let me alone with him:** leave him to me. Cf. iii, 4, 121, 201.—**gull:** trick.—**a nayword:** a byword. She will trick him so thoroughly that his name shall become a proverbial synonym for a 'gull'—a dupe.

150. **Possess us:** inform us.

151–158. **a kind of Puritan.** Maria uses *Puritan* in the loose sense: 'a Puritanical or strait-laced person.' Sir Andrew takes the word in its strict sense as denoting a member of the Puritan party in the Church. Sir Toby's question ('Thy exquisite reason?') is prompted by a desire to hear Sir Andrew dilate on ecclesiastical questions; but Sir Andrew refuses to be drawn. This time he really trumps Sir Toby's trick; and his reply has become a stock justification for refusing to bother about details when one has substantial grounds for action.

159–166. **constantly:** consistently.—**a time-pleaser:** a time-server; a sycophant. Cf. *Coriolanus*, iii, 1, 44, 45: 'call'd them Time-pleasers, flatterers.'—**affection'd:** affected.—**cons state without book:** studies stateliness in language and behaviour until he knows it by heart. Cf. i, 3, 28, 29: 'speaks three or four languages word for word without book'; *Troilus and Cressida*, ii, 1, 18–20: 'I think thy horse will sooner con an oration than thou learn a prayer without book.'—**utters it by great swarths:** expresses it in huge quantities. A *swarth* or *swath* is, literally, that amount of grass, etc., that is mown by one swing of the scythe.—**the best persuaded of himself:** one that has the highest possible opinion of himself.—**it is his grounds of faith:** it is his fixed belief. All the elements of his creed are united in one firm opinion.—**vice:** fault. Cf. iii, 4, 390.

173, 174. **most feelingly personated:** very exactly represented —as by one who describes or depicts a person with the keenest feeling for accuracy.—**on a forgotten matter:** when we no longer remember the subject matter.

185. **Ass.** The standard pun on *ass* and *as*. Cf. *Hamlet*, v, 2, 43; Lyly, *Mother Bombie*, iv, 2 (ed. Bond, III, 212):

> *Stellio.* I wyll talke with Memphios sonne; but as for Riscio—!
> *Memphio.* As for Dromio—!
> *Halfpenny.* Asse for you all foure!

188-190. **let the fool make the third.** When Maria's plot is carried out, Fabian—not Feste—'makes the third' (ii, 5). Such slight changes are common in the plays and need not indicate extensive revision.—**construction:** interpretation.—**the event:** the outcome; the result; the upshot. Cf. iii, 4, 429.

193, 194. **Penthesilea:** Queen of the Amazons. In humorous laudation of the rather diminutive Maria. Cf. i, 5, 218; ii, 5, 15; iii, 2, 71.—**Before me.** A light oath. As *before God!* means 'I swear, taking God to witness,' so *before me!* or *afore me!* means 'I swear, taking myself to witness.' Cf. *Romeo and Juliet*, iii, 4, 34; *Othello*, iv, 1, 149; *Pericles*, ii, 1, 84.

195. **a beagle:** a very small dog noted for its keenness as a hunter.—**one that adores me.** See v, 1, 372.

200. **recover:** win.—**a foul way out:** out of pocket in a very unpleasant fashion—to a very disagreeable extent.

202. **call me Cut:** a dock-tailed horse. Cf. *1 Henry IV*, ii, 4, 213, 214: 'If I tell thee a lie, spit in my face, call me horse'; Gascoigne, *Supposes*, v, 5, 4 (ed. Bond, p. 63): 'And if I be not euen with thee, call me cut'; Jonson, *A Tale of a Tub*, iv, 1, 95-97 (ed. Snell, p. 63): 'If I prove not As just a Carrier as my friend Tom Long was, Then call me his curtall.' The horse often serves as an emblem of stupidity, as in *Troilus and Cressida*, iii, 3, 125, 126: 'Heavens, what a man is there! A very horse, that has he knows not what'; *Julius Cæsar*, iv, 1, 29 ff.; *Much Ado*, i, 1, 68 ff.

206. **burn some sack:** heat some sherry.

Scene IV.

1. **morrow:** morning.

3-5. **ántique:** old-fashioned, quaint. Such dissyllabic adjectives are regularly accented on the first syllable when the next syllable in the verse has an accent. Cf. *ádverse* (v, 1, 87).—**pas-**

sion: love pangs. Cf. l. 97.—**recollected:** 'studied' (Warburton)
—in contrast with the 'plain' style of the old-fashioned song
(l. 44).

12. **father.** The fact that Olivia's father has taken delight in
Feste's foolery explains the privileged position the jester enjoys in her household. Compare what the widowed Countess
in *All's Well* tells Lafew about the clown Lavatch: 'My lord
that's gone made himself much sport out of him. By his authority he remains here, which he thinks is a patent for his
sauciness; and indeed he has no pace, but runs where he will'
(iv, 5, 67-71).

18. **Unstaid and skittish.** Synonymous. To explain or emphasize a word by adding a synonym is a favourite rhetorical device. It should not be confused with faulty repetition. Cf.
ll. 34, 35; i, 1, 12, 13. See *King Lear*, ii, 4, 91, note.—**motions:**
thoughts and feelings. Compare what Orsino says in i, 1, 7-15.

21, 22. **the seat Where love is thron'd:** the heart. It gives the
loving heart a voice that expresses truly what the heart feels. 'It
evokes a response from the very heart' (Child).

25, 26. **stay'd:** lingered.—**favour:** features, face.—**by your
favour.** Viola catches up Orsino's word and plays with it. Orsino
naturally takes 'by your favour' in its ordinary sense, as a courteous formula—'if you please.'

30-32. **still:** always.—**so wears she to him:** thus she adapts
herself to him instinctively.—**So sways she level:** thus she main-
tains an equipoise in the love that her husband bears her.

34, 35. **Our fancies are:** the love that we men feel is. *Fancy*
is very common in this sense. Cf. i, 1, 14; v, 1, 397. The plural
accords with a frequent Elizabethan usage. Abstract nouns are
often pluralized when they refer to more than one person. Cf. v,
1, 73.—**won.** The Folio reads *worne*. Hanmer made the obvious
correction. *Worn*, to be sure, 'makes sense' and has been vig-
orously defended; but *won* is almost inevitable in this context.

38. hold the bent: maintain its intensity—literally, its tension. The figure comes from bending a bow.

40. display'd: full blown.

45–49. spinsters: spinners.—**free:** care-free.—**weave their thread with bones:** weave thread on bone bobbins to make 'bone lace.' Cf. D'Avenant, *News from Plymouth*, ii (ed. 1873, IV, 134):

> Why, he will sing you like any widow's daughter
> That's working of bone lace.

—**silly sooth:** 'plain, simple truth' (Johnson).—**dallies with the innocence of love Like the old age:** expresses a true lover's feelings in such figures as were used in the good old days of childlike sincerity. To *dally* is to 'play' or 'sport.' The word implies that the tragic phrases of the song are not to be taken with literal seriousness: they express feeling rather than thought. Orsino contrasts the straightforward style of the old song with the artificial paradoxes that characterize the love language of his own time. Note, for example, the phrases used by Romeo in describing his love for Rosaline (i, 1, 183 ff.):

> O brawling love! O loving hate!
> O anything, of nothing first create!
> O heavy lightness! serious vanity!
> Misshapen chaos of well-seeming forms!
> Feather of lead, bright smoke, cold fire, sick health!
> Still-waking sleep, that is not what it is!
> This love feel I, that feel no love in this.

Dally and *innocence* suggest also contrast with modern times, which hold (with Rosalind in *As You Like It*, iv, 1, 94–96) that 'the poor world is almost six thousand years old, and in all this time there was not any man died in his own person, videlicet, in a love cause.'

52, 53. **Come away:** Come hither—literally, Come away from where you are.—**cypress:** a coffin of cypress wood.

58, 59. **My part . . . share it:** 'Though *Death* is a *part* in which every one acts his *share*, yet of all these actors no one is *so true* as *I*' (Johnson).

69. **There's.** Emphatic: 'There is payment.' Cf. *Romeo and Juliet*, ii, 4, 194.

72. **pleasure will be paid:** we always have to pay for any indulgence in pleasure. *Will be paid* means 'insists on being paid': *will* is emphatic. The fool's moral reflection is extant in several forms of proverb: e.g., 'Never pleasure without repentance'; 'Pleasure has a sting in its tail'; 'Short pleasure, long lament.' See Tilley, *Elizabethan Proverb Lore*, No. 493; Apperson, *English Proverbs*, pp. 502, 567.

76–81. **doublet:** jacket.—**changeable taffeta:** a kind of thin silk woven of threads of different colours so as to give an opalescent effect.—**opal.** 'A stone distinguished with colors of diuers precious stones. . . . Therein is the firie colour of yᵉ Carbuncle, the shining purple of the Ametistus [i.e., amethyst], the bright greene colour of Smaragdus [i.e., emerald], and all the colours shine therein, with a manner diuersitie' (Batman vppon Bartholome, 1582, xvi, 73, fol. 264 rᵒ; cited by Furness).—**intent:** destination.—**that's it that always makes a good voyage of nothing:** That is the character that is very successful in bringing home a fine cargo of nothing as the result of its voyaging. Feste is a sound philosopher. To achieve anything one must have a constant aim in mind. If your destination is *everywhere*, you get *nowhere*. Cf. Guazzo, *The Civile Conversation*, translated by Pettie, 1586, fol. 63 vᵒ: 'The Prouerbe, That he is not any where, who is euerie where.'

82. **give place:** withdraw, depart.

83. **sovereign:** supreme, transcendant.—**cruelty.** Cf. i, 5, 307. An abstract noun is often used to designate a person. Cf. 'Bring

in the admiration,' i.e., 'this wonderful person' (*All's Well*, ii, 1, 91); 'Bravely, my diligence' (*Tempest*, v, 1, 241). See *Romeo and Juliet*, iii, 5, 237, note.

86–89. The parts . . . her: the qualities and endowments that she owes to fortune—i.e., her rank and riches.—**I hold as giddily as fortune:** I value as slightly as fortune does. Fickle Fortune may at any moment take them away from her, but that would make no difference to *me*.—**that miracle . . . pranks her in:** her own miraculously beautiful self, as Nature has created her—as distinguished from Fortune's gifts. *Nature* is emphatic, as opposed to *Fortune*.—**pranks her in:** adorns her with. She herself is her own adornment, being, as she is, a 'miracle' of beauty.

91. I. The Folios read 'It.' Hanmer made the correction.—**Sooth:** But in very truth. Cf. ii, 1, 11.

95. she. Emphatic: 'that lady.'—**be answer'd:** accept your answer.

97. bide: endure.—**passion.** Cf. l. 4.

99. to hold: as to contain.—**retention:** 'the power of retaining' (Wright).

100. may be call'd appetite: 'as being soon satisfied' (Child).

101, 102. No motion of the liver, but the palate: not a genuine passion but a mere casual liking. The liver was anciently regarded as the seat of the passion of love. Cf. i, 1, 37; iii, 2, 21.[1] *Motion* for 'impulse,' 'emotion,' 'passion' is common. Cf. *Merchant of Venice*, v, 1, 86: 'The motions of his spirit are dull as night'; *Othello*, i, 3, 334, 335: 'our raging motions.'—**suffers:** experiences.—**surfeit:** overeating.—**cloyment:** satiety.—**revolt:** revulsion—the change from appetite or desire to distaste or rejection.

104. can digest as much. Cf. i, 1, 10, 11; *Tempest*, iii, 3, 55: 'the never-surfeited sea.'—**compare:** comparison.

---

[1]See also *Tempest*, iv, 1, 55, 56; *Merry Wives*, ii, 1, 120, 121; *Much Ado*, iv, 1, 232; *As You Like It*, iii, 2, 443–445.

114. **a worm i' th' bud:** a rose canker—the worm that eats
out the inside of the bud and kills the rose. Cf. *Two Gentlemen*,
i, 1, 45, 46: 'The most forward bud Is eaten by the canker ere it
blow.'

115. **damask:** of mingled red and white, like a damask rose.
Cf. *Sonnet* 130:

> I have seen roses damask'd, red and white,
> But no such roses see I in her cheeks.

—in thought: in melancholy brooding. Cf. *Antony and Cleopatra*, iii, 13, 1:

> *Cleopatra.* What shall we do, Enobarbus?
> *Enobarbus.*   Think, and die.

116. **green and yellow:** pale and sallow (in complexion). Cf.
Macbeth, i, 7, 37: 'to look so green and pale.'

117, 118. **like Patience on a monument:** like a monumental
figure of calmness and fortitude.—**Smiling at grief:** bearing her
grief with a smile of resignation. This goes with *she*, not with
Patience.

120. **Our shows are more than will:** What we *show* in our
love-making is greater than the passion that we actually *feel*.—
still: ever, always.

124. **I know not.** Viola still hopes that her brother Sebastian
has not been drowned. See i, 2, 4–21.

127. **can give no place:** cannot give way; must hold its
course.—**bide no denay:** submit to no denial (refusal).

Scene V.

---

1. **Come thy ways:** Come on; come along. *Ways* is, literally,
'on your way.' It is an adverbial genitive.—**Fabian:** a gentleman in the service of Olivia.

2-4. **a scruple:** the least bit—literally, a third of a dram (in apothecary's weight).—**this sport.** Sir Toby has just explained the proposed trick.—**boil'd to death:** an old method of execution for the crime of poisoning. 'Fabian jests; melancholy being a "cold" humour' (Wilson).

6. **sheep-biter:** sneak—literally, a dog that bites sheep. Furness quotes Nashe, *Piers Pennilesse*, 1592 (ed. Grosart, II, 35): 'What curre will not bawle, & be ready to flye in a mans face, when he is set on by his master, who, if hee bee not by to encourage him, he casts his taile betwixt his legges, & steales away like a sheep byter.' Cf. *Measure for Measure*, v, 1, 358, 359: 'Show your sheep-biting face and be hang'd!'

12. **black and blue:** thoroughly—within an inch of his life.

14. **it is pity of our lives.** As we might say now-a-days, 'life won't be worth living.' Literally the phrase means 'it would be a pity about our lives'—i.e., 'our lives would be in danger.' Cf. *Midsummer Night's Dream*, v, 1, 228, 229, where Snug, taking the part of a lion in the play, explains that he is not actually a lion:

> For, if I should as lion come in strife
> Into this place, 'twere pity on my life.

15, 16. **little villain.** Cf. i, 5, 218; ii, 3, 193; iii, 2, 71.—**my metal of India:** my golden girl. *India* means 'the East Indies.'

20-23. **make a contemplative idiot of him:** fill his mind with idiotic meditation. Compare the remarks of Jaques on Touchstone's 'deep contemplative' soliloquy in *As You Like It*, ii, 7, 12 ff.—**Close:** keep in hiding.—**trout . . . tickling.** For this method of catching trout Steevens quotes Cogan, *The Haven of Health*, 1589, p. 143: 'This fishe of nature loueth flatterie; for being in the water it will suffer it selfe to bee rubbed and clawed, and so to be taken.' Halliwell compares Marston, *Antonio and Mellida*, ii, 1, 115-117 (ed. Bullen, I, 34): 'How he

tickles yon trout under the gills! you shall see him take him by
and by with groping flattery': Fletcher, *The Humorous Lieu-
tenant*, iii, 5 (ed. Dyce, vi, 479): 'This is the tamest trout I ever
tickled.' See George H. Kingsley, *Notes on Sport and Travel*,
1900, p. 465.

30–33. **she:** i.e., Olivia.—**did affect me:** was fond of me;
loved me.—**should she fancy . . . complexion:** if she were ever
to fall in love, it would certainly be with a man of my temperament—a staid, sober, dignified person. One's *complexion* (in the
old sense) was thought to be the result of the compounding of
the four humours in the system—blood, phlegm, bile, and melancholy (i.e., black bile—an imaginary substance).—**follows her:**
is in her service.

36. **jets under his advanc'd plumes:** struts like a turkey cock
that elevates his feathers when he is showing off. Cf. *Henry V*,
v, 1, 14, 15: 'Why, here he comes, swelling like a turkey cock.'
Advance often means 'raise.'

37. **'Slight.** An oath 'by God's light!' Cf. iii, 2, 14. See
Genesis, i, 3. Dame Quickly uses the full form, 'God's light,' in
1 Henry IV, iii, 3, 71.

39. **Peace, I say.** The Folios give this to Sir Toby; also, in
l. 43, 'Peace, peace!' Clark and Wright suggested the corrections.

44, 45. **the Lady of the Strachy.** An otherwise unheard-of personage. Some old romantic story is in Malvolio's mind. *Strachy*
may be a misprint, but no satisfactory emendation has been
suggested. See Textual Notes.—**the yeoman of the wardrobe:**
one of a staff of servants in charge of the wardrobe of a noble
family.

46. **Fie on him!** A much stronger curse than in modern usage.
Cf. *Hamlet* i, 2, 135.—**Jezebel.** The cruel and haughty wife of
Ahab, King of Israel (*1 Kings*, xxi, 5 ff.; *2 Kings*, ix, 30 ff.).
'Pride will have a fall!'

48. **blows him:** makes him swell; puffs him up with pride.

Cf. *King Lear*, iv, 4, 27: 'No blown ambition doth our arms incite.'

50. **my state:** my chair of state; 'a chair with a canopy over it' (Steevens). The word also suggests 'stateliness.' Cf. *Macbeth*, iii, 4, 3–5:

> Ourself will mingle with society
> And play the humble host.
> Our hostess keeps her state.

51. **a stone-bow:** 'a cross-bow, a bow which shoots stones' (Johnson).

52–54. **branch'd:** embroidered with figures of branches, leaves, etc.—**a day-bed:** a sofa.

58, 59. **to have the humour of state:** to express in speech and demeanour a majestic disposition.—**after a demure travel of regard:** after surveying the assembled household with a grave and dignified air.

64–66. **make out:** make their way out; leave the room.—**play with my—some rich jewel.** Malvolio is about to say 'with my chain,' when he remembers that he will no longer be a steward or major-domo, and so 'he stops short . . . and alters his phrase to "some rich jewel"' (Nicholson). Cf. ii, 3, 128.

70. **Though . . . by th' ears:** though to keep silence may be a mighty effort. 'By th' ears' is Hanmer's emendation for the Folio reading 'with cars.' Cf. *2 Henry IV*, ii, 4, 313, 314: 'I come to draw you out by the ears.'

73. **with an austere regard of control:** with a stern look of authority.

74. **take you a blow:** give you a blow. Cf. *Richard III*, i, 4, 159, 160: 'Take him on the costard [i.e., the pate] with the hilts of thy sword'; *Taming of the Shrew*, iii, 2, 165: 'took him such a cuff.'

82. **Out.** A common interjection of scorn or anger: 'away

with you!' The modern slang phrase 'get out!' is a direct descendant.—**scab!** vile fellow!

84. patience: be calm; control yourself.

90. employment: business. 'What's going on here?' 'What does this mean?'

92. woodcock ... gin. Cf. iv, 2, 64. The woodcock (though in fact an intelligent bird) was a proverbial symbol of credulous foolishness. It was even thought to fumble with the gin (the snare) in stupid curiosity and thus to achieve its own capture. Cf. *Hamlet*, i, 3, 115; v, 2, 317.

93, 94. the spirit of humours ... to him! May the impulse that governs one's whims suggest to him the idea of reading it aloud!

95–97. her very C's, etc. If anybody in the audience is minutely observant, he may note that there is neither a C nor a P in the address of the letter. Perhaps Malvolio does not read the whole of the address. Ritson was ingenious enough to supply such an omission: 'this, and my good wishes, with *Care Present*.' —**in contempt of question:** so manifestly that it would be absurd to doubt the fact.

103. By your leave, wax. Malvolio addresses the seal, with an apology for breaking it. The phrase was conventional. Cf. *King Lear*, iv, 6, 264; *Cymbeline*, iii, 2, 35.—**Soft!** An interjection of pausing: 'Wait a moment!' Cf. i, 5, 312.

104. Lucrece. The chaste Lucretia, 'attired in mourning garment,' would be a good emblem of Olivia's vow (i, 1, 26–32). See Shakespeare's summary of the story in his introduction to *The Rape of Lucrece*.—**uses:** is accustomed.

106. This wins him, liver and all: This makes a complete conquest of him; is enough to make him passionately in love. See ii, 4, 101, note.

111. The numbers alter'd! More verses, but in a different metre!

114. **Marry.** See i, 3, 71, note.—**brock!** badger. Used as a term of contempt, the badger being a malodorous beast.

118. **doth sway my life.** Cf. *As You Like It*, iii, 2, 4: 'Thy huntress' name that my full life doth sway' (Steevens).

119. **fustian:** nonsensical. Fustian is a kind of coarse cotton cloth.

120. **wench:** girl. Cf. i, 3, 45, note. Sir Toby is admiring Maria's cleverness.

124. **What dish:** What a dish!—**dress'd:** prepared.

125. **staniel:** kestrel—an inferior species of hawk.—**checks at it.** A falcon is said to *check* 'when she forsakes her proper game, and follows some other of inferior kind that crossed her in her flight' (Dyce on *Hamlet*, iv, 7, 63). Cf. iii, 1, 71. Sir Toby means: 'How readily the silly fellow is attracted by this nonsense and led astray from the truth in his attempt to interpret it!'

128–131. **to any formal capacity:** to any normal understanding; to anybody who has a normal mind.—**no obstruction in this:** no difficulty about the meaning of this.—**Softly!** Cf. l. 103.

133–136. **make up that:** fit *that* together; make sense out of *that*.—**He is now at a cold scent:** He is now attempting to follow the hare when the scent is cold—i.e., to solve a riddle which is too hard for him.—**Sowter . . . fox:** The dog will have a try at it, nevertheless, though the deceit is as obvious as the smell of a fox. *Sowter* is the name of a hound. It means, literally, 'cobbler,' and may or may not be intended to suggest clumsiness or stupidity. To *cry upon't* is, literally, to 'give tongue' like a hound that discovers the scent of the animal he is hunting.

139,140. **excellent at faults.** A *fault* is a 'break in the scent.' Fabian is punning. He appears to praise Malvolio for skill in following the game, even when the scent is cold; but he implies that, in fact, Malvolio is a first-rate follower-up of false trails—sure, therefore, to get the full benefit of the trick they are playing on him.

141, 142. there is . . . sequel . . . probation: there is no consistency in what follows. That breaks down when one tests it.

145. O: lamentation. Steevens compares *Romeo and Juliet*, iii, 3, 90: 'Why should you fall into so deep an O?'

149. any eye behind you. Fabian alludes (with a phantom pun) to the symbolic figure of *Prudence*, which has three eyes—one in the back of the head. Cf. Chaucer, *Troilus*, v, 744–749.— **149, more detraction at your heels:** more defamatory speech in pursuit of you.

151-154. This simulation: this veiled indication; this expression of a hidden meaning.—**the former:** i.e., 'I command where I adore'—which was very easy to understand.—**to crush this a little, it would bow to me:** if I should use a little force with this 'M, O, A, I,' it would yield and come into agreement with *me*—would signify *me*, Malvolio.—**Soft!** See i, 5, 312, note.

155-167. revolve: consider.—**my stars:** my lot in life; my rank and fortunes.—**open their hands:** offer bounteous gifts Cf. *Troilus and Cressida*, iv, 5, 100, 101:

> His heart and hand both open and both free,
> For what he has he gives, what thinks he shows.

So *open-handed* means 'generous.'—**let thy blood . . . them:** accept their offers with the whole strength of thy nature.— **inure:** accustom.—**like:** likely.—**cast thy humble slough:** throw off thy garb of lowliness as a snake casts his old skin.— **tang . . . state:** sound forth matters of public policy (statecraft) in thy talk. Cf. *Richard II*, iii, 4, 27: 'They will talk of state.' To fulfil this injunction Malvolio determines to 'read politic authors'—i.e., books that deal with statesmanship (l. 170).— **singularity:** peculiarity—almost equivalent to 'eccentricity.'— **cross-garter'd:** with 'hose garters going acrosse, or ouerthwart, both aboue and beneath the knee' (Junius, *Nomenclator*, English edition, 1585, quoted by Douce). Such garters would be particularly conspicuous.—**Go to.** A common interjection of impatience or protest. See i, 5, 45, note.—**alter services with thee:** make thee her master and become thy servant.

169–192. **champian:** champaign; open country.—**discovers:** discloses, reveals—'This is as plain as day.'—**politic authors:** writers on statecraft and political subjects, from whose works I can learn 'arguments of state.'—**baffle:** treat contemptuously; put down. Cf. v, 1, 377. To *baffle* was, literally, to 'degrade one from knighthood.' See *1 Henry IV*, i, 2, 113 (and note): 'Call me villain and baffle me.'—**gross:** low, vulgar.—**point-devise:** exactly what the letter advises—to a T. *The very man* repeats this idea.—**to let imagination jade me:** by letting my imagination trick me. *Jade* is a contemptuous term for a worthless or tricky horse. Malvolio means that he is not deluded by his imagination but has good evidence that Olivia loves him.—**excites to this:** prompts me to this conclusion.—**in this . . . liking:** in this letter she reveals herself as wishing to be loved by me and, as it were, imposes on me the duty of adopting this costume that she likes.—**happy:** fortunate.—**strange:** haughty. *Stout* is practically synonymous.—**Jove.** For Feste the Jester to invoke Jove (i, 5, 121; iii, 1, 50) is highly appropriate. Here, however (and in l. 185; iii, 4, 80, 91; iv, 2, 13), it is possible that Shakespeare wrote 'God' and that, before the play was printed, 'Jove' had been substituted in obedience to the Statute of 1606 forbidding the profane use of the name of God on the stage.—**canst not choose but know:** cannot help knowing.—**entertain'st:** acceptest.

198. **the Sophy:** the Shah of Persia. Cf. iii, 4, 307. The 'pension of thousands' may allude (as Farmer suggests) to Sir Robert Shirley's return from that country (in 1599) with rich gifts from the Shah.

203. **Nor I neither.** Cf. iii, 1, 171; v, 1, 364.

204. **gull-catcher.** A *gull* is a young bird, a nestling; then,

figuratively, a person easily cheated, a dupe. Cf. iii, 2, 73; v, 1, 213, 351.

207. **play:** stake—and lose.—**tray-trip:** an old gambling game, played with dice.

210, 211. **when the image of it leaves him:** when he awakes and the vision fades away.

215. **aqua-vitæ:** distilled liquor; brandy or whiskey. The word *whiskey* is a clipped form of the Irish phrase *uisce baugh*, 'water of life.'

225. **Tartar:** Tartarus; hell.

227. **I'll make one too:** I'll accompany you.

ACT III. Scene I.

1, 2. **Save thee:** God save thee. Cf. l. 76.—**live by:** get thy living by.—**tabor:** a small drum. Tabor and pipe were the regular musical equipment of a jester.

4. **a churchman:** an ecclesiastic; a clergyman. Viola plays up to the jester, giving him a chance to explain his joke.

5. **No such matter:** nothing of the kind; not at all; by no means.

7. **lies by:** lodges or dwells near—with an obvious pun.

12, 13. **You have said:** You have made your point.—**A sentence:** any expression of a fact or opinion.—**a chev'ril glove.** Cheveril was a kind of light and flexible kid. Cf. *Romeo and Juliet*, ii, 4, 87.

16, 17. **They that dally nicely with words . . . wanton:** Those who play subtly with words (making fine distinctions) can soon make the words ambiguous. *Dally* often means to 'toy amorously' and *wanton* often means 'unchaste.' Viola, then, is suggesting a pun, and Feste picks up the suggestion and goes on 'dallying with words.'

25. **bonds disgrac'd them:** because now we have to make a man give his bond if we are to feel sure that he will keep his promise. A man's 'word' is no longer 'as good as his bond.'

27–29. **Troth:** literally, 'by my pledged faith.' Cf. i, 3, 3.—**yield:** give.—**words.** Feste continues his pun on *word* in the sense of 'promise.'—**to prove reason with them:** to test the reasonableness of any proposition by means of words. Feste puns on *reason*, which Viola has used in the sense of 'the reason for your statement.'

30. **car'st for nothing:** feelest no anxiety about anything; dost never worry.

32–35. **in my conscience:** to tell you precisely my inmost thoughts; to confess the truth to you.—**you.** Emphatic.—**to care for nothing:** to care for something is the same as not to care for nothing; then perhaps the fact that I do not care for *you* makes you equivalent to *nothing*; and, in that case, I wish you might be actually nothing, and so—invisible.

38–41. **till she be married.** The regular joke—that husbands are always befooled by their wives.—**pilchers:** pilchards—a kind of small fish. Cf. Nashe, *Lenten Stuffe*, 1599 (ed. Grosart, V, 257): 'Cornish Pilchards . . . are but counterfets to the red Herring as Copper to Golde.'—**corrupter of words.** A witty definition of the kind of foolery that has so far occupied Feste and Viola in this scene.

43–47. **the orb:** this round earth.—**I would be sorry.** *Would* for *should* is common in Elizabethan English.—**but:** but that.—**your wisdom.** A title imitated from 'your honour,' 'your lordship,' etc. Thus Feste ironically suggests that Viola is as big a fool as *he* is.

48, 49. **an thou pass upon me,** etc.: if you mean to make thrusts at me (with your witticisms), I'll have no more talk with you.—**expenses:** spending money.

50. **Jove.** See ii, 5, 190, note.—**commodity:** lot.

52. **sick for one:** lovesick for a certain man.

55. **a pair of these.** Thus Feste suggests that he should like to have another coin to match that which Viola has given him.

56. **put to use:** put out at interest.

57. **Pandarus.** Cressida's uncle, who brought Troilus and Cressida together.

59. **well:** skilfully, adroitly.

61–65. **The matter . . . is not great:** It is not a great piece of begging. We need not suppose (with Wilson) that Feste implies that Viola's gratuity is unduly small. He is merely defending himself from any accusation of exorbitant begging and, incidentally, leading up to the culmination of his reference to Cressida.—**a beggar.** In Robert Henryson's poem *The Testament of Cressid*, a continuation of Chaucer's *Troilus and Cressida* (included in sixteenth-century editions of Chaucer), Cressida is turned adrift by Diomedes, becomes a common harlot in the Greek camp, is smitten with leprosy, and is forced to beg by the roadside. Thus Pistol calls Doll 'the lazar [i.e., leper] kite of Cressid's kind' (*Henry V*, ii, 1, 80).—**conster:** construe, interpret, explain.—**welkin.** *Welkin* means 'the sky,' and *element* often had the same meaning (cf. i, l, 26). Hence Feste's elegant pun, which modern English cannot reproduce. He means 'beyond my comprehension.'

67–75. **wise enough to play the fool.** This speech is enough to show that Feste is not a 'natural'—a born fool—as most of the jesters were in old times, but (like Touchstone) a clever fellow who has taken up folly as a profession. See *As You Like It*, Introduction, pp. xiii–xvi.—**wit:** mental agility; cleverness.—**observe:** adapt himself to.—**quality.** This word suggests 'rank' as well as 'quality in general.'—**the haggard:** a wild or untrained hawk.—**check at every feather:** fly off heedlessly at every bird he sees—i.e., make personal jests without discrimination. For *check at* see ii, 5, 125, note.—**a practice:** a piece of professional skill.—**fit**: fitting, proper.—**folly-fall'n**: when they fall into folly—foolish speech and conduct.—**taint their wit**: disgrace their natural wisdom.

76. **Save you.** Cf. l. 1.

77. **And you, sir.** The conventional reply to such a greeting. Cf. i, 3, 50, 51; iii, 4, 238, 239. So Horatio replies to the Sailor's 'God bless you, sir': 'Let him bless thee too' (*Hamlet*, iv, 6, 6, 7). Cf. *King Lear*, ii, 1, 1, 2.

81, 82. **encounter**: approach,—literally, 'meet.' Sir Toby uses comically elevated language.—**trade**: business.

85. **bound.** Explained in the next sentence. *Trade* suggests to Viola the figure of a *voyage*.—**list**: limit, destination.

87. **Taste**: make trial of. 'See what your legs can do in the way of walking.' This sense of *taste* was common enough (cf. iii, 4, 265, 266: 'to taste their valour'; *1 Henry IV*, iv, 1, 119: 'Come, let me taste my horse'); but, in the context, *taste* sounds so grotesque that Viola pretends to be puzzled. Thus she scores—in the game of mild witticisms—by forcing Sir Toby to explain.

90, 91. **My legs . . . mean**: My legs *stand under* me well enough; but I do not *understand* your remark. Cf. *Two Gentlemen*, ii, 5, 25 ff.:

> *Speed.* I understand thee not.
> *Launce.* What a block art thou that thou canst not! My staff understands me.
> *Speed.* What thou say'st?
> *Launce.* Ay, and what I do too. Look thee, I'll but lean, and my staff understands me.
> *Speed.* It stands under thee indeed.
> *Launce.* Why, stand-under and under-stand is all one.

93. **I will answer . . . entrance**: I will reply in accordance with your explanation—by *going* and *entering*.

94. **prevented**: forestalled, anticipated. *Prevent* in Shakespeare regularly keeps the force of *pre-*.

95. excellent: excellently.

99, 100. My matter ... ear: My errand must not be disclosed, lady, except to your own ear—if you will condescend to show readiness to listen. *Pregnant* often means 'ready.'

102. ready: i.e., to use in my own talk.

109–111. 'Twas never merry world ... Orsino: This world has never been a pleasant place to live in since it became the fashion to call one's self 'servant' as a mere term of ceremony. You are not my servant, but the Count Orsino's. ''Twas never merry world' is an old conventional phrase used in contrasting the present day with the good old times. So John Holland, one of Jack Cade's rebels, declares that 'it was never merry world in England since gentlemen came up' (*2 Henry VI*, iv, 2, 9, 10).— **lowly feigning:** 'an affectation of humility' (Wright).

112. he is yours: *your* servant. *Servant* was a conventional term for 'suitor,' as *mistress* was for 'lady-love.' So Richard, in his courtship of Lady Anne, styles himself her 'poor devoted servant' (*Richard III*, i, 2, 206).

114. For: As for.

117. by your leave: allow me. A courteous phrase of interruption: 'Pray let me speak.'

118. I bade you never speak again of him. See i, 5, 299: 'I cannot love him. Let him send no more.'

121. music from the spheres. The stars were supposed, in their revolution about the earth, to give utterance to a superb harmony, which mortals cannot hear. Cf. *Merchant of Venice*, v, 1, 60–65:

> There's not the smallest orb which thou behold'st
> But in his motion like an angel sings,
> Still quiring to the young-ey'd cherubins;
> Such harmony is in immortal souls;
> But whilst this muddy vesture of decay
> Doth grossly close it in, we cannot hear it.

122. **beseech:** I beseech.

123–125. **enchantment.** Cf. i, 5, 315–317. Viola uses the same figure (ii, 2, 19): 'Fortune forbid my outside have not charm'd her!'—**abuse:** deceive.—**you.** Emphatic. Olivia fears that Cesario may have misinterpreted her character.

126–128. **Under ... sit:** I must, I fear, have subjected myself to very harsh judgment on your part. *Construction* is, literally, 'interpretation.'—**To force:** by forcing.—**in a shameful cunning:** by a trick that was disgraceful.—**none of yours:** not yours at all.—**might:** could.

129–130. **at the stake.** The figure comes from bear-baiting. The bear was tied to a stake and the dogs were set on to attack him. Cf. i, 3, 100. To *bait* means, literally, to 'cause [the dogs] to bite [the bear].' Cf. *Macbeth*, v, 7, 1, 2, and note.

131. This line is an alexandrine (twelve syllables) with an extra syllable at the end: 'That týr|annous heárt | can thínk? | To óne | of yoúr | receív|ing.'—**tyrannous:** cruel, savage.—**To one of your receiving:** to one as quick of apprehension as you.

132. **cypress:** a veil of black crape—almost transparent.

133. This appears to be a nine-syllable verse, the first foot consisting of one emphatic syllable. Such verses abound in the older Elizabethan drama, and there is no good reason for supposing that Shakespeare always avoided them. Several editors read 'Hideth' to regularize the metre. Dover Wilson arranges the line-endings of ll. 131–135 as follows: 'think,' 'shown,' 'heart,' 'pity you,' 'grize,' 'proof.'

134, 135. **degree, grize.** Synonymous: 'step.' Cf. *As You Like It*, v, 2, 41, 42: 'In these degrees have they made a pair of stairs to marriage'; *Othello*, i, 3, 199–201:

> Let me speak like yourself and lay a sentence
> Which, as a grise or step, may help these lovers
> Into your favour.

—**a vulgar proof:** a thing of ordinary experience.

137, 138. **'tis time to smile again:** it is time for me to dismiss
these love-pangs from my mind—if he is my enemy. Olivia is
talking to herself rather than to Viola.—**If one should be a
prey . . . wolf:** If I had to be a prey to love, would it not have
been better to fall in love with my noble suitor Orsino than with
this hard-hearted youngster?—**apt:** ready.

143–146. **when . . . harvest:** when you are mature in age and
wisdom. Olivia implies that Cesario is too young to know what
is good for himself.—**proper:** handsome.—**due west:** toward
the setting sun—with a suggestion that she is dismissing him
from her favourable thoughts. Viola replies with the call of the
Thames boatmen when bound to the westward.

147. **Grace:** the favour of heaven.—**good disposition:** a happy
frame of mind.

148. **You'll nothing?** You do not wish to send any reply?

151. **That you do think you are not what you are:** that you
think you are in love *with a man*, not with a woman. Of course
Olivia cannot understand this riddle. She takes the words to
mean: 'that you are out of your senses without knowing it,' and
retorts: 'And so, I think, are you, or you would accept my love.'

156. **I am your fool:** you are making a fool of me. Viola pretends to think that Olivia is not in earnest; but she really means
that she herself is put in a ridiculous position by Olivia's wooing.

160. **love's night is noon:** All attempts to conceal one's love
make it only the more evident.

163. **maugre all thy pride:** in spite of the scorn you show.

165–168. **Do not extort . . . better:** Do not draw forced arguments for your action in this case from the proposition that,
because I offer my love unsought, you have no reason to accept
it; but, on the contrary, attach firmly one proposition to another, and so conclude that 'love sought is good, but given unsought is better.'

171. **nor never none:** nor ever any one. Cf. ii, 5, 203.

Scene II.

2. **venom.** An abstract noun for a concrete. See ii, 4, 83, note.

5. **yield:** give. Cf. iii, 1, 27.

6–9. **Marry.** See i, 3, 71, note.—**orchard:** garden—not limited, as in modern usage, to a plantation of fruit trees. *Orchard* is a form of *wort-yard*.

12. **argument of love in her:** evidence to prove love on her part.

14. **'Slight.** See ii, 5, 37, note.

15. **legitimate:** legitimately—i.e., as it were, legally, by the sworn testimony of judgment and logical reasoning.

17. **grand-jurymen:** and therefore good judges of evidence.

20–31. **dormouse:** sleepy, dormant.—**valour:** courage as a suitor.—**brimstone in your liver:** i.e., to heat it. The liver was regarded as the seat of the passion of love. See ii, 4, 101, note. —**fire-new:** brand-new.—**this was balk'd:** this opportunity was missed.—**an icicle on a Dutchman's beard.** Barentz, a Dutchman, had made a voyage to the Arctic regions which was famous when TWELFTH NIGHT was written. An account of his discoveries and of the hardships his men suffered was entered for copyright in the Stationers' Register in 1598 (Arber, III, 118).— **policy:** strategy.

34. **Brownist:** a member of the religious denomination founded by Robert Browne (b. *ca.* 1550, d. *ca.* 1633). They were opposed both to the Episcopal and the Presbyterian form of church government and adopted that form now called Congregational. Sir Andrew, who was hostile to the Puritan party (ii, 3, 151–158), was of course even more horrified by Brownist principles.—**politician:** Sir Andrew has taken *policy* in the sense of 'political trickery.' Cf. *King Lear*, i, 2, 48.

35, 36. **me.** The so-called 'ethical dative.' It adds nothing to the sense but gives a light touch to the style. Cf. iii, 4, 190.—**to fight with him:** i.e., offering to fight with him.

39. **love-broker:** agent in love matters; go-between.—**can:** that can.

45–53. **curst:** ill-tempered, cross.—**so:** provided that; if only.—**with the license of ink:** with all the freedom in language that written speech allows.—**If thou thou'st him:** if you use *thou* instead of *you* in your letter. *Thou* was the pronoun of familiar address and was therefore common in insulting language. See Sir Andrew's letter (iii, 4, 161 ff.). Theobald compares Coke's style in attacking Sir Walter Raleigh when on trial for treason in 1603: 'by thy instigation, thou viper; for I thou thee, thou traitor.'—**the bed of Ware:** a famous bedstead—one of the sights of Shakespeare's time; now in Rye House near Ware in Hertfordshire. It is more than ten feet wide.—**gall.** Oak galls were used in ink-making. Cf. *Cymbeline*, i, 1, 101. The pun on *gall*, 'bitterness,' is obvious.—**with a goose-pen:** a goose quill, such as was regularly used for a pen. Sir Toby implies that Sir Andrew will write in a foolish style. Cf. iii, 4, 202–210.

56. **cubiculo:** cubicle; the chamber or private room where you are to write the letter.

57–58. **a dear manikin to you:** a little man that you like to play with as if he were a puppet. Sir Toby catches up the word *dear* and applies it in the sense of 'costly,' 'expensive.'—**some two thousand.** Cf. ii, 3, 200, 201.

64–67. **wainropes:** wagon ropes.—**hale:** haul.—**For:** as for.—**blood in his liver.** Fear was supposed to be caused by lack of blood in the liver. Hence *white-livered* for 'cowardly.' Cf. *Macbeth*, v, 3, 15: 'Thou lily-liver'd boy'; *2 Henry IV*, iv, 3, 111 ff.: 'The second property of your excellent sherris [i.e., sherry] is the warming of the blood; which before (cold and settled) left the liver white and pale, which is the badge of pusillanimity and cowardice.'—**th' anatomy:** his dissected body. Since *anatomy* sometimes means 'skeleton,' Sir Toby may be alluding to Sir Andrew's thin frame. Cf. *Comedy of Errors*, v, 1, 237, 238: 'a hungry lean-fac'd villain, A mere anatomy.'

68. **opposite:** opponent. Cf. iii, 4, 254, 292.

71. **nine.** 'The Wren is remarkable for laying many eggs at a time, nine or ten and sometimes more: and as she is the smallest of birds, the last of so large a brood may be supposed to be little indeed, which is the image here intended to be given of Maria' (Hanmer). Cf. i, 5, 218; ii, 3, 193; ii, 5, 15. *Nine* is Theobald's emendation for the Folio reading, *mine.*

72–78. **If you desire the spleen.** Explained by the synonymous phrase that follows: 'If you wish to laugh yourselves into a fit— to laugh till you have stitches in your sides.' Laughter was supposed to be caused by the action of the spleen. Cf. *Troilus and Cressida*, i, 3, 176–178:

> O, enough, Patroclus,
> Or give me ribs of steel! I shall split all
> In pleasure of my spleen.

—**gull:** dupe. Cf. ii, 5, 204, note.—**renegado:** renegade, apostate—one who 'turns traitor.'—**such impossible passages of grossness:** such grossly (obviously) impossible statements (as those in the letter). *Gross* is, literally, 'big'; then, 'manifest,' 'obvious.' Cf. *1 Henry IV*, ii, 4, 249, 250: 'These lies are . . . gross as a mountain, open, palpable.' *Passages* often means 'facts' (as in *Hamlet*, iv, 7, 113)—and so, here, 'alleged facts,' which are really impossibilities.

80. **pedant:** pedagogue.

83, 84. **the new map . . . Indies:** a map prepared by Edward Wright and others which shows the East Indies as well as North America in an augmented form—that is, in a fuller delineation than in any previous map. See C. H. Coote, *New Shakspere Society Transactions*, 1877–79, p. 88; J. D. Rogers, *Shakespeare's*

England, I, 173, 174. The lines are the rhumb lines in the map—
each of which 'crosses successive meridians at a constant angle'
(Webster). Cf. Greene, *Alcida* (ed. Grosart, IX, 17): 'Her face
full of wrinkles, furrowed so with age, as in her visage appeared
the very map of antiquitie.'

Scene III.

1–3. See ii, 1, 1–3, 35 ff.—**by my will:** willingly.

6–9. And not all love to see you, etc.: and it was not merely
my fondness for your company that 'spurred me forth'—though
that was great enough to induce me to make a longer journey—
but also anxiety about what might befall you in your wanderings.
—**skilless:** unacquainted.

12. The rather . . . fear: made all the more willing by these
considerations urged by fear.

16–18. shuffled off: put aside; rewarded inadequately.—
uncurrent pay: payment in coin that does not pass current—for
thanks are mere *words*, not *deeds*.—**my worth:** my wealth. Cf.
Romeo and Juliet, ii, 6, 32: 'They are but beggars that can count
their worth.'—**my conscience:** my consciousness of my in-
debtedness to you.—**dealing:** payment.

18, 19. What's to do? What's to be done? What shall we do to
pass the time?—**the relics:** the antiquities; the ancient buildings
and monuments. Lines 22–24 give fuller expression to the idea.

24. pardon me: excuse me (from going with you to see the
sights).

26–28. the Count his galleys: the Count's ships of war.—**it
would scarce be answer'd:** I should find it hard to justify myself
in his eyes.

29. Belike: Perhaps; very likely. Cf. iii, 4, 266.

31–36. Albeit: although.—**bloody argument:** cause for bloodshed.—**answer'd:** settled.—**for traffic's sake:** in order to resume trade relations with the city.—**lapsed:** taken when off my guard; surprised. A *lapse* is a 'slip,' a 'heedless mistake': cf. 'a lapse of memory'; to 'slip up.'

39. **the Elephant.** A well-known inn sign in Shakespeare's day.

41. **Whiles:** while.

42. **have me:** find me whenever you wish.

44–46. **toy:** trifle. Cf. v, 1, 400.—**your store . . . markets:** your supply of money is not large enough for unnecessary spending.

Scene IV.

1–5. **him:** Cesario.—**he says he'll come:** suppose he consents to come.—**of him:** on him.—**sad and civil:** serious-minded and sedate. Cf. ii, 3, 133.

9–14. **possess'd:** i.e., with a devil; distracted. Insanity or delirium was often ascribed to demoniacal possession. See *Comedy of Errors*, iv, 4, 48 ff.—**were best.** Cf. i, 5, 33; ii, 2, 27.—**in's:** in his.

20. **sad:** serious. Malvolio picks up the word and echoes it in the sense of 'gloomy in expression.'

24, 25. **sonnet.** Often used for any form of short lyric.—**'Please one, and please all':** If I can please *one* (the one that I love), that is enough for me—I am satisfied. An appropriate motto for a devoted lover. Halliwell identifies it as the title of a poem copyrighted in 1592 (Arber, *Transcript*, II, 602): 'A prettie newe Ballad, intytuled: The Crowe sits vpon the wall, Please one and please all.' The first stanza runs:

> Please one and please all,
> Be they great be they small,

> Be they little be they lowe,
> So pypeth the Crowe,
>> sitting vpon a wall:
>> please one and please all,
>> please one and please all.

The poem is signed 'R. T.'—perhaps for 'Richard Tarlton.' See J. Lilly, *A Collection of Seventy-nine Black-letter Ballads and Broadsides*, 1867, 1870, pp. 255–259; Rollins, *Analytical Index*, 1924, No. 429.

   31. **Roman hand.** An Italian style of handwriting, much like modern script. It was fashionable, especially with ladies, when *Twelfth Night* was written. The old 'secretary hand' (much less legible) was still in use. Compare the jest of King James's fool, Archie Armstrong: 'A question being asked, why women, either all, or the most part, when they learne to write, practise Romane hand; it was answered [by] him againe, that it stood with great reason, for he had never heard of any woman that made good Secretary' (*A Banquet of Jests and Merry Tales*, ed. 1889, p. 57).

   35. **God comfort thee!** God sustain thee!—i.e., support thy crazed wits, restore thee to sanity.

   38. **At your request? . . . daws!** Am I to give an account of my health at the request of a servant like you? 'Yes, indeed,' he adds, ironically, 'for that would be as reasonable as for a nightingale to reply to the call of a jackdaw!'

   46. **Ha?** The ordinary interrogative—'huh?' Cf. iv, 2, 85.

   54. **My.** The Folio reads 'Thy.' Lettsom suggested the correction.

   57. **Go to.** See i, 5, 45, note.

   61. **midsummer madness.** Midsummer was traditionally a mad season. Midsummer Eve (June 23) was thought to be a magic time and was celebrated with ancient rites. See *Midsummer Night's Dream*, Introduction, pp. ix, x.

   70. **miscarry:** come to harm.

71–89. **do you come near me now?** do you get some idea who I am?—what an important person?—**stubborn.** The best explanation of this word is given by Malvolio's treatment of Sir Toby in ll. 99, 100.—**tang:** sound.—**consequently:** as a logical consequence. Malvolio says that Olivia, by exhorting him to put himself into a 'trick of singularity,' implied (though she did not express) the way in which he was to appear and act.—**sad:** serious.—**habit:** attire. Cf. ii, 5, 177; v, 1, 223, 396.—**some sir of note:** some distinguished personage.—**lim'd:** caught. 'I have entangled or caught her, as a bird is caught with birdlime' (Johnson). *Birdlime* is a sticky substance smeared on the branches of trees. Cf. *Hamlet*, iii, 3, 68, 69: 'O limed soul, that, struggling to be free, Art more engag'd!'—**Jove's doing.** Luce compares *Psalm* cxviii, 23: 'This is the Lord's doing; it is marvellous in our eyes.' See ii, 5, 190, note.—**after my degree:** according to my rank.—**fellow:** Malvolio takes this word in the sense of 'companion' or 'associate.' Cf. *Henry V*, v, 2, 261: 'fellow with the best king.'—**adheres together:** coheres; is consistent.—**no dram of a scruple,** etc. Malvolio begins by using *dram* in the general sense of 'little bit' and *scruple* in the sense of 'doubt'; but the words suggest to him the terms of apothecaries' weight, and so he adds (in emphasis) 'not even a *scruple* of a scruple'—'no scruple, however scrupulous.' In apothecaries' weight three scruples make one dram.—**incredulous:** incredible. —**unsafe:** risky (as evidence); dubious; doubtful.

95. **be drawn in little:** should be portrayed in miniature—i.e., were brought together in possessing this one man.—**Legion.** An allusion to the demoniac in *Mark*, v, 8, 9: 'He [Jesus] said unto him, Come out of the man, thou unclean spirit. And he asked him, What is thy name? And he answered, saying, My name is Legion: for we are many.'

99. **discard you:** cast you off; refuse to associate with you.— **private:** privacy.

105–108. Go to. See i, 5, 45, note.—**Let me alone:** Leave him
to me; don't interfere! Sir Toby proceeds to 'deal gently with
him,' and speaks in a comically coaxing tone.—**defy:** renounce.
Cf. *King Lear*, iii, 4, 102: 'Defy the foul fiend.'

111. La you: 'Lo!' 'Just see!'

113. bewitch'd. Demoniacal possession is (in strictness) something different from bewitchment; for a demon, it was thought,
could take possession of one without the agency of a witch. But
in popular belief the two things were confused, and possession
was often ascribed to a witch's spells. See Kittredge, *Witchcraft
in Old and New England*, pp. 134 ff., 297 ff.

114. Carry . . . woman: i.e., for medical diagnosis. A wise
woman was the respectful term for a 'good witch'—one who
acted as a physician in ordinary diseases and was skilful in the use
of charms that would cast out devils and relieve one from the
spells of witchcraft. Cf. *2 Henry IV*, i, 2, 1, 2; *Macbeth*, v, 3, 50–
54; *Merry Wives*, iv, 2, 77 ff.; iv, 5, 12 ff. Thomas Heywood's
play *The Wise-Woman of Hogsdon*, iii (cited by Douce), gives a
lively picture of a wise woman's activities: 'Let mee see how
many Trades I have to live by: First, I am a Wise-woman, and
a Fortune-teller, and under that I deale in Physicke and Fore-
speaking [i.e., prophesy], in Palmistry, and recovering of things
lost. Next, I undertake to cure Madd folkes' (Pearson ed.,
V, 310).

121. move: excite.—**Let me alone with him:** Leave him to
me to manage. Cf. ii, 3, 146.

126. bawcock, chuck. Familiar terms of affection. *Bawcock*
(*beau coq*) is masculine, *chuck* ('chick') usually feminine. Such
language of course rouses Malvolio almost to fury and so makes
him appear all the more a madman.

128–130. Ay, biddy, come with me. Still in Sir Toby's comical
parody of a gentle, coaxing style. *Biddy* is still common as a
childish name for a hen or chicken.—**'Tis not . . . Satan:** It is

not proper for a dignified person like you to take Satan for a playfellow. *Cherry-pit* was a child's game in which the players pitched cherry-stones into a little hole. Steevens quotes *The Witch of Edmonton*, iii, 1 (Ford, ed. Gifford and Dyce, 1869, III, 216): 'I have loved a witch ever since I played at cherry-pit,' i.e., ever since I was a child.—collier. Dr. Johnson's explanation is, as usual, satisfying: 'The devil is called Collier for his blackness; "Like will to like like," says the Devil to the Collier.' This proverb is quoted in Baret's *Alvearie*, 1580 (A, No. 589). See Apperson, *English Proverbs*, p. 367. *Collier* was the regular term for a 'pedlar of small coals.'[1] Greene gives 'A Pleasant Discovery of the cossenage of Colliers' in his tract entitled *A Notable Discovery of Coosnage*, 1591 (ed. Harrison, pp. 51–55).

136, 137. idle: foolish.—I am not of your element: I belong to a higher sphere than you. Cf. iii, 1, 65, and note.

142. His very genius. The *genius*, in Elizabethan usage, commonly means a guardian spirit, inseparable from the man himself and sharing his fortunes (cf. *Antony and Cleopatra*, ii, 3, 19–30). Here, however, 'his genius' is practically equivalent to 'his ego,' 'his ruling personality.' See *Julius Cæsar*, ii, 1, 66–69, and note.

144, 145. take air and taint: be exposed to the air (revealed) and so spoiled.

148-155. in a dark room and bound. The regular expert treatment for insanity in old times. See *Comedy of Errors*, iv, 4, 95–97:

> Mistress, both man and master is possess'd.
> I know it by their pale and deadly looks.
> They must be bound and laid in some dark room.

Cf. *As You Like It*, iii, 2, 420, 421: 'Love is merely a madness, and, I tell you, deserves as well a dark house and a whip as mad-

[1] *A Knacke to Know an Honest Man*, 1596 (Malone Society ed., ll. 1382 ff., 1408 ff.).

men do.' Cf. iv, 2, 44, and note.—**carry it:** manage it; carry out the plot.—**to the bar:** i.e., to be judged.—**a finder:** a finder out; a detector.

156. More matter for a May morning: Here is more subject matter for a comic May-day drama.

159. saucy? With a pun on the literal meaning of the word—'highly spiced.'

160. Ay, is't, I warrant him: Yes indeed it is, I can assure him (Cesario).

161, 162. thou. It will be noted that Sir Andrew has followed and improved upon Sir Toby's suggestion about *thou* (iii, 2, 47, 48).—**scurvy:** vile—literally, scurfy, scabby.

164. admire. A synonym for *wonder*.

168, 169. A good note! A good point!—**That keeps you . . . law:** since you bring no definite charge against him, you cannot be accused of defamation of character, *scurvy* being a mere vague epithet. Cf. *Romeo and Juliet*, i, 1, 45 ff.

181. o' th' windy side of the law: to the windward of the law and therefore not exposed to its blasts. Cf. *Much Ado*, ii, 1, 325.

183, 184. my hope is better. Thus Sir Andrew ludicrously expresses the hope that he shall not be killed in the duel.—**as:** according as—i.e., thy friend insofar as thou treatest me in friendly fashion.

188, 189. occasion: opportunity.—**in some commerce:** in conversation about some business or other.—**by-and-by:** very soon.

190–200. me. Ethical dative. See iii, 2, 35, note.—**orchard:** garden. Cf. iii, 2, 9.—**like a bum-baily:** as if you were a bailiff (sheriff's officer) lurking there to arrest him as soon as he should leave the premises.—**gives manhood . . . him:** gives a man more reputation for courage than any actual test of his valour would have won for him.

201. let me alone: don't worry about me on that point—you may trust me for swearing! Cf. ii, 3, 146.

210–215. **a clodpoll:** a dunce; a stupid fellow—literally, one who has a clod of earth for a head.—**as . . . receive it:** as [well I may, for] I am sure the gentleman's youth and inexperience will make him ready to accept my report as the truth. For *as* in ellipsis cf. i, 2, 32; v, 1, 246, 272.—**cockatrices:** basilisks. A fabulous serpent with a cock's head; it killed by the venomous glance of its eye. Cf. *Romeo and Juliet*, iii, 2, 46, 47:

> That bare vowel 'I' shall poison more
> Than the death-darting eye of cockatrice.

217. **Give them way:** Let them go on without interference.

218. **presently after him:** then follow him immediately.

222–224. **laid mine honour too unchary out:** made too lavish an expenditure of my honour in trying to win your love. Olivia feels that her outspoken wooing of Cesario (iii, 1, 161 ff.) has been out of accord with womanly modesty. *Out* is Theobald's correction of the Folio reading ('on't').—**potent:** powerful.

226. **haviour:** behaviour.

231. **deny:** refuse.

232. **That . . . give:** that honour can grant at your request without being infringed.

233. **Nothing but this:** I will ask nothing of you except *this*.

235. **acquit you:** release you from your offer of love.

237. **like thee:** in thy shape.

239. **And you, sir.** The regular conventional response. See iii, 1, 77, note.

240–245. **defence:** skill in fencing. Cf. *Hamlet*, iv, 7, 97, 98: 'such a masterly report For art and exercise in your defence.'—**despite:** angry defiance.—**bloody:** bloodthirsty. Cf. *Macbeth*, iv, 1, 79: 'Be bloody, bold, and resolute.'—**the hunter:** a hunting dog; a hound on the trail. Cf. *Macbeth*, iii, 1, 97.—**Dismount thy tuck:** unsheathe thy rapier. Sir Toby uses grandiloquent language—as if the rapier were a cannon.—**yare:** ready; on the alert.

247, 248. **quarrel to me:** cause of quarrel with me.

254–255. **opposite:** opponent. Cf. l. 292; iii, 2, 68.—**what:** whatsoever.—**withal:** with. Very common in this sense at the end of a clause.

257–262. **with unhatch'd rapier and on carpet consideration:** not for military service but for reasons connected with the affairs of peace. *Unhatch'd* is, literally, 'unhacked.' *Carpet* is opposed to battlefield. *Consideration* suggests that Sir Andrew's service was a gift of money to some influential person. As to *carpet knights*, Francis Markham, *The Booke of Honour*, 1625, p. 71 (cited by Reed), tells us that the term was used because 'they receiue their honour from the Kings hand, in the Court, and vpon Carpets.' Cf. Edward Hall's *Chronicle* (ed. 1809), p. 56: 'Men effeminate, more mete [i.e., meet, fit] for a Carpet then a Campe'; *Captain Thomas Stukeley*, 1605 (ed. Simpson, I, 201): 'Thou know'st I am a soldier And hate the name of carpet-coward to death.' Nashe, *The Terrors of the Night*, 1594 (ed. McKerrow, I, 353), describes carpet knights as 'the basest cowards vnder heaven' and as 'couering an apes hart with a lions case.'—**incensement:** anger.—**Hob, nob.** The original meaning seems to have been 'Have it, or have it not!' This accords with Sir Toby's translation: 'Give it, or take it!' Other forms are *hab*, *nab* and *hab or nab*. The implication is that Sir Andrew's only terms are an immediate contest—hand to hand.—**word:** watchword, motto.

263–266. **conduct:** escort.—**of:** from.—**taste:** test. Cf. iii, 1, 87.—**Belike:** probably. Cf. iii, 3, 29.—**quirk:** peculiar habit; eccentric fashion.

268–276. **competent:** sufficient, adequate.—**undertake that:** i.e., a duel.—**answer him:** undertake in accepting *his* challenge. *Me* and *him* are emphatic.—**meddle:** engage in the affair; fight.

—**forswear . . . about you:** renounce your claim to wear a sword; admit that you are a coward and no fit associate for gentlemen.

277–279. **uncivil:** discourteous.—**this courteous office, as to know of the knight:** so courteous a service as to learn from the knight.—**something of my negligence:** some oversight on my part; something unintentional.

285, 286. **even to a mortal arbitrement:** to such an extent that only death can settle the matter.—**circumstance:** circumstances.

290–292. **to read:** to interpret, to judge.—**proof:** test, experience.—**opposite:** opponent. Cf. l. 254; iii, 2, 68.

298, 299. **go with:** associate with.—**sir priest.** *Sir* (i.e., *Dominus*) was a priest's title. See iv, 2, 2: 'Sir Topas the curate.' —**my mettle:** my constitution.

301–307. **firago:** virago. Sir Toby applies this feminine term, for comic effect, to one whom he supposes to be a man; but the audience, aware that Cesario is a woman, enjoys both the joke and the mistake. *F* for *v* doubtless indicates merely a common pronunciation of Shakespeare's time, like *fagaries* for *vagaries* and *fat* for *vat*.—**a pass:** a bout—literally, a thrust.—**the stuck-in:** the stoccado or stoccata; the thrust. Cf. *Hamlet*, iv, 7, 162; *Romeo and Juliet*, iii, 1, 77, note.—**on the answer:** at the return; when he parries a thrust he gives you a thrust in return. —**the Sophy:** the Shah of Persia. See ii, 5, 198, note.

308. **Pox on't.** A common curse: 'plague take it!'—**meddle with him:** have anything to do with him. Cf. l. 275.

313–315. **cunning:** skilful, expert.—**Capilet.** *Capil* or *capul* is an old term for 'horse' and *Capilet* (as Wright suggests) seems to be a diminutive of this word. See *New English Dictionary*, s.v. *caple*.

316–320. **the motion:** the proposal; the offer.—**the perdition of souls.** Merely Sir Toby's high style for 'loss of life.' Cf. *Tempest*, i, 2, 30: 'Not so much perdition as an hair.'—**take up:**

settle (without a duel). See Touchstone's burlesque on the elaboration with which 'quarrels' were 'ta'en up' (*As You Like It*, v, 4, 51 ff., 71 ff.).

322. **is as horribly conceited:** has as horrible an idea.

325–329. **for 's oath sake:** for the sake of his oath. *Oath* instead of *oath's*—the two *s's* coalescing, as often.—**his quarrel:** his cause of offence.—**draw . . . vow:** draw your sword to enable him to keep his oath.

336, 337. **one bout:** one exchange of thrust and parry. Cf. *Hamlet*, v, 2, 295: 'I'll play this bout first.'—**by the duello:** in accordance with the rules of honour that gentlemen must observe in the matter of duels. These rules are elaborately set forth in a work published in 1595: *Vincentio Saviolo his Practice*. The author was famous. Cf. Dekker, *The Wonderfull Yeare 1603*, D3 v⁰ (ed. Harrison, p. 56): 'Hees the best Fencer in the world: *Vincentio Sauiolo* is no body to [i.e., in comparison with] him.'

345. **If you offend him:** if it is *you* that have given him cause of offence.

350. **if you be an undertaker:** if you wish to take up the matter—to undertake responsibility in this affair. Cf. *Othello*, iv, 1, 224: 'As for Cassio, let me be his undertaker'—i.e., 'leave him to me to settle with.' For *undertake* in the sense of 'undertake a fight with' see *Cymbeline*, ii, 1, 28–30: 'It is not fit your lordship should undertake every companion that you give offence to.'

352. **I'll be with you anon.** Sir Toby sheathes his sword but promises Antonio to fight with him at the first opportunity.

356, 357. **for that I promis'd you:** as for my promise to give you my horse.—**reins:** minds the rein.

359. **do thy office:** perform thy function (as an officer).

362. **favour:** features, face. Cf. l. 416.

367. **I shall answer it:** i.e., make what defence I can to the charge the Duke brings against me and submit to my sentence.

371. **amaz'd:** in a maze; bewildered. A very strong word. Cf. v, 1, 271; *Midsummer Night's Dream*, iii, 2, 344: 'I am amaz'd, and know not what to say.'

377–381. **part:** partly.—**My having:** what I have.—**my present:** my cash in hand.—**my coffer:** my store of money.

383, 384. **persuasion:** 'persuasive efficacy' (Child).—**tempt:** put too hard a test upon; try too severely.—**Lest that:** lest. See i, 2, 48, note.—**so unsound a man:** so lacking in manly dignity and self-control; so unmanly.

389, 391. **vainness:** untrustworthiness—not, vanity.—**babbling:** lack of the power to hold one's tongue in confidential matters—not, mere talkativeness.—**vice:** in the general sense of 'fault.' Cf. ii, 3, 166.—**blood:** human nature.

395–397. **such.** This merely emphasizes the meaning of *sanctity*.—**to his image:** 'to what he appeared to me to be' (Child). Cf. l. 399.—**Most venerable worth:** worthiness of devout reverence.

400. **feature:** form and features.

401, 402. **In nature . . . unkind:** No natural blemish in a man's *body* can be called a blemish. The word can be applied only to one's *mind* or *disposition*; for unkindness is the only real deformity. Antonio is thinking especially of ingratitude. Cf. *As You Like It*, ii, 7, 174–176:

> Blow, blow, thou winter wind,
> Thou art not so unkind
> As man's ingratitude.

404. **empty trunks . . . the devil.** Chests for clothing, etc., ornamented with carving or painting, were features of old-fashioned house-furnishing.—**empty:** because they have no good qualities of heart or mind. Their beauty is all external; it is given them by Satan as a delusion and a snare.

407, 408. **passion:** intense feeling.—**he believes himself; so do not I:** This man believes his own assertion—i.e., that I am my

brother Sebastian; but I cannot yet trust the hope that his words
give me that Sebastian is alive.

412. **sage saws:** wise moral maxims—like those which this
stranger has been uttering.

415-418. **living in my glass:** whenever I look in my mirror, I
see my brother's image to the life.—**favour:** features. Cf. l. 362.
—**Still:** always.—**prove:** if my hope prove true.

421. **dishonest:** dishonourable. Cf. iv, 2, 35.

425. **religious in it:** as if he had taken a vow to devote himself to cowardice.

426. **'Slid:** literally, 'by God's eyelid.' Many such grotesque
oaths were in use. They were uttered without much thought of
their literal meaning. See Chaucer, *The Pardoner's Tale*, C 651 ff.
(ed. Robinson, p. 183).

429. **the event:** the outcome; the upshot of the affair. Cf. ii,
3, 190.

430. **lay:** bet, wager.—**yet:** after all.

Act IV. Scene I.

---

3. **Go to!** An interjection of protest. See i, 5, 45, note.

5-9. **Well held out!** Well maintained! Feste declares ironically that Sebastian shows excellent perseverance in refusing to
admit that he is Cesario.—**nor this is not my nose neither:** 'It is
as plain that you are Master Cesario as that this [*points to his
nose*] is the nose on my face' (Tilley, *Philological Quarterly*, VI
[1927], 309). Cf. *Two Gentlemen*, ii, 1, 140, 141:

> O jest unseen, inscrutable, invisible,
> As a nose on a man's face or a weathercock on a steeple!

See Apperson, *English Proverbs*, p. 452.

10. **vent thy folly:** utter thy foolish talk. *Vent* for 'utter'
occurs often enough in Shakespeare. Cf., for example, 'They

vent reproaches' (*Henry VIII*, i, 2, 23); 'They vented their com-
plainings' (*Coriolanus*, i, 1, 213). Feste does not ridicule the term
itself: he merely makes fun of it as inappropriate in familiar talk.

12–15. **of:** with reference to.—**I am afraid . . . a cockney:** I
fear the whole stupid world will turn out to be as silly as may be.
Since you talk so foolishly, I despair of finding common sense
anywhere in creation.—**ungird thy strangeness.** Feste is imita-
ting the elaborate style that he pretends to have detected in
Sebastian's 'vent.' He means, 'Let thyself loose from thy pre-
tence of not being Cesario and not understanding my message.'

19. **Greek:** nonsensical talker—because what you say is Greek
to me. *Greek* for 'unintelligible language' is common enough.
Cf. *Julius Cæsar*, i, 2, 286, 287: 'it was Greek to me'; Greene,
James IV, iv, 2 (ed. Collins, II, 131): ''Tis Greeke to mee, my
Lord.' *Greek* may also suggest 'jester.' Cf. *Troilus and Cressida*,
i, 2, 118: 'Then she's a merry Greek indeed!' Collier reminds us
that Matthew Merrygreek is a character in Udall's *Ralph Roister
Doister*.

24, 25. **report:** reputation (as reported by the fools).—**after
fourteen years' purchase:** but it is a long time before they get
that reputation from the fools. To buy land at the price of
'fourteen years' purchase' is to pay in cash what the rent of the
land (its annual return) will amount to in fourteen years. This
was a high price for land and it would certainly be a long delay
for a good reputation!

29. **I'll throw your dagger o'er the house.** This indicates that
Sebastian has drawn his dagger and used it to beat Sir Toby—
not, manifestly, to stab him. For this use of a dagger see *Romeo
and Juliet*, iv, 5, 118, 119: 'Then will I lay the serving-creature's
dagger on your pate'; *Henry V*, iv, 1, 54–57:

Pistol. Tell him I'll knock his leek about his pate Upon Saint Davy's day.
King. Do not you wear your dagger in your cap that day, lest he knock
that about yours.

32. straight: straightway, immediately.—**I would . . . two-pence.** See Tilley, *Philological Quarterly*, VI (1927), 306, 307.

34. Come on, sir; hold! Addressed to Sebastian, who is struggling to free himself from Sir Toby. *Come on* means 'Come along'—away from Sir Andrew.

36, 37. I'll have . . . battery: I'll bring him to trial for assault and battery.—**stroke:** struck.

41, 42. Come, sir, . . . Come on. All this is manifestly addressed to Sebastian, who is struggling in Sir Toby's grasp. Some editors insist that 'Come, my young soldier, put up your iron. You are well flesh'd' is addressed to Sir Andrew. Nothing can be clearer, however, than that Sir Andrew has not drawn his sword. He has given Sebastian a buffet, expecting no resistance. See iii, 4, 426, 427:

> *Andrew.* I'll after him again and beat him!
> *Toby.* Do; cuff him soundly, but never draw thy sword.

—**put up your iron:** sheathe your dagger.—**You are well flesh'd:** You have had a good taste of fighting. To *flesh* means to give a dog a taste of raw meat in order to make him fierce.— **Come on:** Come along with me—away from Sir Andrew.

45. tempt me: make trial of me; try my mettle.

47. malapert: saucy.

51. Ungracious: graceless.

55. Rudesby: quarrelsome fellow; ruffian. Cf. *Taming of the Shrew*, iij, 2, 10, where Katherine describes Petruchio as 'a mad-brain rudesby, full of spleen'—i.e., ill temper.

56, 57. fair: i.e., using fair judgment.—**sway:** rule.—**uncivil.** Much stronger than in modern usage—almost equivalent to 'barbarous,' 'outrageous.' Cf. *Two Gentlemen*, v, 4, 17: 'uncivil outrages.'—**extent:** exhibition (of violence), display.

60. botch'd up: clumsily contrived and managed.

61–63. Thou shalt not choose but go: I insist on your going with me.—**deny:** refuse.—**Beshrew:** literally 'curse,' but in common use a mild and ladylike term.—**for me!** on my account. —**heart.** With an allusion to *hart.* Cf. i, 1, 16 ff.

64-67. What relish is in this? 'How does this taste? What judgment am I to make of it?' (Johnson).—**Or . . . or:** either . . . or.—**fancy:** imagination.—**still:** ever, always.

Scene II.

2, 3. Sir. See iii, 4, 298, note. *Sir Topas* (i.e., Topaz), the burlesque parish priest, seems to take his name from Chaucer's burlesque knight Sir Thopas.—**the whilst:** in the meantime.

4-12. dissemble myself: disguise myself. Feste chooses the word for the sake of the pun on *dissemble*—'hide one's true character'; 'conceal the truth about one's self.'—**the function:** the priestly office. Cf. v, 1, 164.—**student:** a common old by-form of *student.*—**said:** called, styled.—**goes as fairly:** sounds as well; is quite as respectable.—**careful:** studious, as befits a clergyman.—**the competitors:** my associates in this plot.

13. Jove. See ii, 5, 190, note.

16-18. the old hermit of Prague. A character invented by Feste. Cf. ii, 3, 21 ff.—**King Gorboduc:** a famous king of ancient British legend. He has a leading part in a once-popular tragedy by Thomas Sackville and Thomas Norton,—*Gorboduc* or *Ferrex and Porrex* (1562).

22. knave: fellow—literally, boy (cf. German *knabe*).

29. hyperbolical. A technical term in rhetoric ('exaggerated in style'), used by Feste as an elegant word for 'raging,' 'turbulent.'

35, 36. dishonest: dishonourable. Cf. iii, 4, 421.—**modest:** moderate, mild. *Dishonest* is a milder term than the outspoken word *liar.* Satan is 'the father of lies.'

40, 41. **barricadoes:** barricades.—**clerestories:** the windows in the upper part of the wall.

44. **house.** 'A darkened room was sometimes called a dark house' (Halliwell). Cf. *As You Like It*, iii, 2, 420, 421: 'Love is merely a madness, and, I tell you, deserves as well a dark house and a whip as madmen do'; Marston, *What You Will*, v, 1, 42, 43 (ed. Bullen, II, 406): 'Shut the windows, darken the room, fetch whips; the fellow is mad: he raves.' Such was the expert treatment of insanity in Shakespeare's day. Cf. iii, 4, 148, and note.

47, 48. **the Egyptians in their fog.** See *Exodus*, x, 21–23.

53. **in any constant question:** on any consistent subject—any subject that calls for rational speech on my part.

54. **Pythagoras:** the Greek philosopher who was regarded as having originated or taught the doctrine of the transmigration of souls. This theory was a matter of common knowledge, but Shakespeare had doubtless read the appropriate passages in Ovid's *Metamorphoses*, xv, 165–175, 456–462. Cf. *As You Like It*, iii, 2, 187; *Merchant of Venice*, iv, 1, 131–133.

56. **happily:** haply, perchance.

62–64. **allow of thy wits:** approve thy intellect as sound.— **a woodcock.** Reputed to be a silly bird. Cf. ii, 5, 92.

68. **Nay.** Merely an interjection, like 'Why.'—**I am for all waters:** 'I can turn my hand to anything' (Malone). The origin of the phrase is obscure; perhaps it meant, 'I am ready for any voyage.'

73–75. **deliver'd:** released.—**to the upshot:** to its conclusion; to the last detail. *Upshot* is, literally, 'the final shot' in archery.

78–85. Feste, now acting *in propria persona* (for he has discarded the beard and gown of Sir Topas), sings part of an old song which begins:

> A [i.e., ah] Robyn,
> Joly Robyn,

> Tell me how thy leman [i.e., lady-love] doeth,
> And thou shalt knowe of myn.
>
> My Lady is vnkynd, perde,
> Alack! why is she so?
> She loveth an other better then me;
> And yet she will say no.

The song has been ascribed to Sir Thomas Wyatt. See Flügel, *Anglia*, XII (1889), 241, 242, and *Neuenglisches Lesebuch*, I, 23. —**perdie!** assuredly. An oath (*par dieu*), but always lightly used.—**ha?** The interrogative interjection—'huh?' Cf. iii, 4, 46.

92. **how fell you besides your five wits?** How did you happen to lose your mind? The 'five wits' (mental faculties), as enumerated by Stephen Hawes (*The Pastime of Pleasure*, xxiv), are common wit, imagination, fantasy, estimation, and memory.— **besides:** out of. Cf. *Much Ado*, v, 1, 127, 128: 'Very many have been beside their wit.' We still use 'beside one's self' for 'out of one's head,' 'distracted.'

95. **notoriously abus'd:** notably ill used. Cf. v, 1, 387.

99–101. **propertied me:** made me a mere thing or utensil—a mere tool, as opposed to 'a person.' In the language of the theatre, tables, chairs, and other movable articles used in fitting out the stage are called *properties*. Thus, Malvolio says, they have used him as a mere lifeless thing in playing their game. Cf. *Julius Cæsar*, iv, 1, 39, 40.—**to face me out of my wits:** shamelessly to insist (in defiance of the obvious truth) that I am a madman. Cf. v, 1, 91.

102, 103. **Advise you:** Consider with yourself; be careful.— **Malvolio.** Here Feste resumes the part of Sir Topas.

105. **vain bibble babble:** senseless babbling; foolish chatter.

107–109. **Maintain . . . I will.** Feste plays both parts—Sir Topas's and his own.—**God b' wi' you:** Good-bye.—**Marry, amen.** Sir Topas's conclusion of his prayer 'Thy wits the heavens restore!' (l. 104). *Marry* is here used with some sense of its original meaning. See i, 3, 71, note.—**I will, sir, I will.** In assent to some order that he pretends Sir Topas has given him.

111. **patient:** calm.—**shent:** scolded, rebuked (by Sir Topas).

116. **Well-a-day that you were, sir!** Alas, sir, I wish you were!

122. **do you but counterfeit?** are you only pretending?

134. **the old Vice:** the comic character in the old morality plays—impersonating Iniquity in general or some particular sin. Cf. Nashe, *Strange Newes*, 1592 (ed. McKerrow, I, 275): 'In this Sonnet you have counterfeited the stile of the olde Vice in the Morals.'

135–141. **Your need to sustain:** i.e., to lend you my assistance in your contest with the devil that possesses you.—**dagger of lath:** the Vice (like the fool in real life) was sometimes armed with a wooden dagger. Cf. *1 Henry IV*, ii, 4, 150–152.—**aha!** a defiant interjection.—**Pare thy nails.** The Vice shows his dagger to Satan and offers to pare his nails. Cf. *Henry V*, iv, 4, 75, 76: 'This roaring devil i' th' old play, that every one may pare his nails with a wooden dagger'; Jonson, *The Staple of News* (Yale ed., p. 54): 'I'ld not giue a rush for a Vice, that has not a wooden dagger to snap at euery body he meetes.'—**Adieu, goodman devil.** Thus Feste bids good-bye to the devil that possesses Malvolio, and so to Malvolio himself. Some editors adopt Rowe's reading *Drivel*, i.e., 'fool,' 'idiot'; but no change is needed or desirable.—**Goodman.** A title appropriate for a person below the rank of gentleman. It was an insult to the devil, for 'the prince of darkness is a gentleman' (*King Lear*, iii, 4, 148).

Scene III.

6, 7. **was.** Emphatic: 'had been.'—**there I found this credit ... out:** there I found that this was what they believed—that he was roaming about the town in search of me.

9–15. **though my soul disputes . . . I am mad:** though my reason agrees with my senses in arguing that my present experiences are real and actual and not an insane delusion, even if they are the result of some error on the lady's part (some mistake that she has made about my identity), yet this flood tide of good fortune that has come to me is so unexampled, so far beyond all reason, that I can hardly trust my eyes and I am ready to disagree with my reason when it tries to make me believe that I am not insane.—**instance:** example.—**discourse:** reason.

18, 19. **Take and give back affairs and their dispatch:** take affairs and give back their dispatch—i.e., receive reports on matters of business and give directions for their management. —**stable:** settled, steady.

21. **deceivable:** deceptive, misleading.

24. **the chantry by:** the chapel that is near by. A *chantry* is a chapel supported by an endowment for the maintenance of a priest or priests to sing daily mass for the souls of designated persons.

26–31. **Plight . . . faith:** give me full assurance of your fidelity by the ceremony of betrothal. See the Priest's description of the ceremony (v, 1, 159 ff.). Cf. v, 1, 268–270.—**jealous:** a common form of *jealous*—a synonym for *doubtful.*—**Whiles . . . note:** until you consent that our betrothal shall be made public. —**What time:** when—i.e., and at that time; and then.—**our celebration:** the public ceremony of our marriage.—**According to my birth:** with such splendour as befits my high birth.

35. **fairly note:** mark with their favour; show that they approve. Olivia's prayer is prompted by a scruple of conscience. She hopes that the Lord will forgive her for breaking her vow (i, 1, 26–32).

Act V. Scene I.

7, 8. **to give a dog . . . my dog again.** Cf. John Manningham's *Diary*, March 26, 1603 (ed. Camden Society, p. 148): 'Mr. Francis Curle told me howe one Dr. Bullein, the Queenes kinsman, had a dog which he doted one, soe much that the Queene understanding of it requested he would graunt hir one desyre, and he should have what soever he would aske. Shee demaunded his dogge; he gave it, and "Nowe, Madame," quoth he, "you promised to give me my desyre." "I will," quothe she. "Then I pray you give me my dog againe."' This amusing anecdote was noted by Miss Emma Phipson (see *Notes and Queries*, IV [1887], 185).

19–26. **and make an ass of me:** fool me by making me think well of myself.—**abused:** deceived, deluded.—**conclusions to be as kisses . . . my foes.** Thus Feste explains his paradox: 'In the matter of kissing, since a girl's refusal is really coy consent, two *no! no!'s* (which are two refusals but count up to four negatives) permit two kisses. If, then, negatives make affirmatives in kissing, I may apply the same principle with regard to friendship and conclude that my non-friends (my foes) are really my friends and *vice versa*—so that I am the worse for my friends and the better for my foes.'—**your four negatives.** *Your* is here (as often) an indefinite pronoun without any possessive sense. It merely gives a colloquial touch to the style. Cf., for example, *As You Like It*, v, 4, 63, 64: 'Rich honesty dwells . . . in a poor house, as your pearl in your foul oyster.'

29. **By my troth.** See ii, 3, 3, note.

32. **But that:** but for the fact that.—**double-dealing.** The pun on *deal* in the sense of 'give' is manifest. The ordinary meaning of *double-dealing* is 'duplicity,' 'trickery,' 'cheating.'

35, 37. **Put your grace in your pocket . . . obey it:** Never mind if I *am* giving you evil counsel! Pocket up (lay aside, repress) your virtue for once in your life and let your human nature follow my advice. Feste puns on *grace* as a title and in the sense of 'favour': 'Let your Grace's favour toward me apply itself to your pocket for another gratuity.'—**to:** as to.

38–41. **Primo, secundo, tertio.** This appears to be an allusion to a childish game. Reginald Scot (*A Discovery of Witchcraft*, 1584, xi, 10, p. 198) characterizes a certain kind of divination as 'a childish and ridiculous toie, and like vnto childrens plaie at *Primus secundus*, or the game called The Philosophers table' (quoted by Wilson).—**The third pays for all.** An old maxim equivalent to 'The third time never fails.' See Apperson, *English Proverbs*, p. 626.—**triplex:** triple time in music.—**Saint Bennet:** Saint Benedict. Some think that Shakespeare was referring to Saint Bennet's Church at Paul's Wharf, near the Globe Theatre; but we are at liberty to imagine a church in Illyria dedicated to this same saint.

44. **fool:** get by your arts as a jester—with a pun on *fool* in the sense of 'cheat.'—**at this throw:** at this throw of the dice; at this stage of the game. The Duke has lost money on the first two 'throws' and he declines to follow the gambler's superstition that the third throw will make up for everything.

57, 58. **A baubling vessel:** a mere plaything in the way of a ship. *Bauble* for 'toy' or 'trifle' is common. *Bauble* (or *bable*) *boat* was a term for a vessel of slight tonnage. Cf. *Troilus and Cressida*, i, 3, 34–37:

> The sea being smooth,
> How many shallow bauble boats dare sail
> Upon her patient breast, making their way
> With those of nobler bulk!

For shallow draught ... unprizable: of little account because of its slight draught and small size.

59–61. scathful: destructive.—**bottom:** ship.—**very envy:** even enmity; even we, his enemies.—**loss:** us, the losers in the battle.

64. fraught: cargo.—**from:** on her voyage from.—**Candy:** Candia—Crete.

67, 68. desperate of shame and state: in utter disregard both of such shameful conduct as to engage in a street brawl and of his dangerous situation as a public enemy. Compare Antonio's own words: 'I do not without danger walk these streets' (iii, 3, 25).—**brabble:** a brawl.—**apprehend:** arrest. Cf. l. 89.

70. put strange speech upon me: addressed me in extraordinary language.

72. Notable: notorious.—**thief:** robber. A much stronger word than in modern usage.

73, 74. mercies. For the plural see ii, 4, 34, note.—**Whom.** The antecedent is implied in *their* (= *of those*).—**in terms so bloody and so dear:** by conduct involving such bloodshed and such intense hostility. *Dear* is very common as an emphasizing adjective. Cf. i, 4, 25.

78. base and ground. Synonymous.

84. retention: holding back.

85–87. All . . . dedication: devoted all-in-all to him.—**pure:** purely, solely.—**ádverse:** hostile. For the accent see ii, 4, 3, note.

91–94. to face me out of his acquaintance: to deny, with shameless effrontery, that he knew me. Cf. iv, 2, 100, 101: 'to face me out of my wits.'—**had recommended to his use:** had handed over to him to use as his own.

97. three months. This is inconsistent with any time scheme that can be made out for the drama, but such difficulties never suggest themselves to an audience.

101. for thee: as for thee.

104. but that he may not have: except what I cannot grant him—i.e., my love.

109. **Good my lord.** *My lord* and similar vocative phrases are often treated as a compound word and preceded by an adjective. Cf. i, 5, 68.

112. **fat and fulsome.** Synonyms: 'nauseous.'

115. **uncivil.** A much stronger word than in modern usage—almost equivalent to 'cruel' or 'barbarous.' Cf. ii, 3, 133; iv, 1, 57.

116. **ingrate:** ungrateful, thankless.—**unauspicious:** refusing all favour; obstinately unpropitious.

121. **th' Egyptian thief.** A reference (as Theobald noted) to the story of *Theagenes and Chariclea* in the *Æthiopica* (i, 30, 31; ii, 5, 6, 14), a Greek novel by Heliodorus. Thyamis, an Egyptian robber chieftain, in love with his captive, Chariclea, is in danger of death or capture, and, fearing she may be taken from him, kills a Grecian woman whom he mistakes for her in the darkness of the cave where she was imprisoned. See the English version by Thomas Underdowne, *An Æthiopian Historie*, ed. Whibly (from the edition of 1587), pp. 38, 48.

125. **that:** since that; since. Cf. i, 2, 48, note.

126. **screws:** forces.

128-131. **minion:** darling.—**I tender dearly:** I hold dear.—**in his master's spite:** as if in despiteful defiance of his master.

135. **apt:** readily. One *-ly* does duty for three adverbs.

139. **by all mores:** by all possible standards of comparison.

140, 141. **you witnesses above:** you heavenly powers.—**for tainting of my love:** for hypocrisy in my protestations of love.

142. **Ay me detested!** Alas for me—cast off with a curse! Cesario has rejected her as a wife by the oath that he has just taken (ll. 137–141).

144. **forgot thyself?** forgotten who thou art? forgotten that thou art my husband? Cf. l. 150.

148. **sirrah.** A form of *sir:* used in familiar address, sometimes in speaking to a servant or an inferior, sometimes in contempt

or reproof, sometimes (as to children) in more or less jocose affection. Cf. l. 290.

150. **strangle thy propriety:** choke thine own identity by denying that thou art thyself—my husband.

153. **As great as that thou fear'st:** as high in rank as the Duke.

156. **To keep in darkness.** See iv, 3, 28–31.

163, 164. **compâct.** Regularly so accented in Shakespeare.— **in my function:** in the regular exercise of my priestly office. Cf. iv, 2, 9.

167. **dissembling.** Cf. iv, 2, 4, note.

168. **a grizzle on thy case:** mingled dark and grey hair on thy skin. Cf. *Hamlet*, i, 2, 240–242. *Case* was the regular term for the skin of a fox. Halliwell quotes *Florio's Second Frutes*, 1591, p. 105: 'And if the Lyons skinne doe faile, Then with the Foxes case assaile.' Furness quotes the pun of the Shepherd's son in *The Winter's Tale*, iv, 4, 843–845: 'Though my case be a pitiful one, I hope I shall not be flay'd out of it.'

169, 170. **Or . . . overthrow?** or else will not your craftiness develop so rapidly that, while you are still a beardless boy, you will destroy yourself in some attempt at trickery?—literally, your attempt to trip up somebody (in wrestling) shall cause you to be thrown yourself?

174. **little:** a little; some little.

175. **presently:** immediately.

178, 179. **Has:** he has. Cf. ll. 201, 292.—**broke my head:** broken the skin of my head—drawn blood.—**coxcomb:** pate.

184. **gentleman:** gentleman in waiting, attendant.

185. **incardinate:** for *incarnate*—'in the flesh,' 'in human shape.' Sir Andrew seldom blunders in his use of words, but here panic makes him stammer a little and thus he gives *incarnate* an extra syllable.

188. **lifelings:** a diminutive of *life*, reducing the sonorous oath 'by God's life' to a ladylike asseveration. Cf. Rosalind's ''Od's

my little life' (*As You Like It*, iii, 5, 43), Imogen's "Od's pitti-kins' (*Cymbeline*, iv, 2, 293), and Slender's "Od's heartlings' (*Merry Wives*, iii, 4, 59).

192. **bespake you fair:** addressed you courteously.

194–199. **set nothing by:** think nothing of.—**halting:** limp-ing.—**othergates:** otherwise.

201–202. **That's all one!** That makes no difference! Never mind about that! Cf. ll. 380, 416; i, 5, 137.—**there's th' end on't:** that's the whole story.—**sot:** fool. Cf. i, 5, 130.

203. **agone:** ago.

206. **a passy measures pavin.** The *pavin* was a stately dance. *Passy measures* is Sir Toby's form for *passamezzo*,[1] a slow tune. He means to call the surgeon 'a grave and solemn humbug.'

210. **be dress'd:** have our wounds dressed.

212, 213. **you.** Scornfully emphasized.—**coxcomb:** fool.—**knave:** fellow.—**thin-fac'd:** See i, 3, 46, note.—**gull:** dupe. Cf. ii, 5, 204, note.

218, 219. **with wit and safety:** with a sensible regard for my own safety. Hendiadys.—**a strange regard:** an estranged (of-fended) look.

223. **habit:** costume. Cf. l. 396; ii, 5, 177; iii, 4, 79; see iii, 4, 414–418.

224. **A natural perspective, that is and is not!** Perspective glasses were optical toys which distorted the shapes of objects or otherwise misrepresented them. Orsino means that, in the present instance, nature not art gives the effect of an optical illusion—makes us see something that we cannot believe to exist. Cf. Hoby, *The Courtier* (ed. *Tudor Translations*, p. 17): 'Without setting-furth the truth with beawtifull coulours, or makinge it appeere by the art of Prospective that [i.e., what] it is not.'

[1]Cf. Middleton, *More Dissemblers Besides Women*, v, 1, 161, 162 (ed. Bullen, VI, 465): 'I can dance nothing but ill-favouredly, A strain or two of passa-measures galliard!'

226. **rack'd and tortur'd.** Synonymous.

228. **Fear'st thou that?** Why are you actually shocked to recognize me? The question is prompted by Antonio's air of amazement.

234, 235. **that deity . . . Of here and everywhere:** that quality of omnipresence, which belongs to God alone.

237. **Of charity:** I pray you to be so kind as to tell me. Literally, *of charity* means 'out of kindness.'

241, 242. **suited:** clad, clothed.—**suit:** costume.

244, 245. **in that dimension grossly clad:** clothed in that bodily form of material substance.—**participate:** derive, inherit.

246. **as the rest goes even:** as [may well be the case, for] all the other circumstances accord with your being my sister. See i, 2, 32, note.

253. **recórd:** recollection, memory.

256. **lets:** hinders. Cf. 'without let or hindrance.' This is the Anglo-Saxon *lettan*, a different verb from the ordinary *let* (A.-S. *lǣtan*).

259. **cohere and jump.** Synonymous: 'coincide,' 'agree.'

262. **weeds:** garments. Cf. l. 280.

267. **nature to her bias drew:** your nature followed its inborn tendency. A figure from bowling. The *bias* is the 'curve' which the bowl takes.—**in that:** in your mistake in taking a maid for a man.

271. **amaz'd:** in a daze. Cf. iii, 4, 371, note.

272, 273. **as . . . true:** as [so it appears to be, for] the perspective glass still seems to be showing reality—not a deceptive appearance. Cf. l. 224.—**wrack:** the wreck mentioned in ll. 235–241.

275. **like to me:** as much as you loved me.

276. **over:** over again; in repetition.

278. **that orbed continent:** the sun. Literally, 'that spherical container (of fire).' *Fire* is the object of the verb 'doth [keep].'

282, 283. **upon some action:** in consequence of some law business.—**in durance:** imprisoned; under arrest.

285. **enlarge:** release.

288–290. **A most extracting frenzy ... his:** A madness of my own, which violently drew me out of my wits, completely banished *his* attack of madness from my memory. Malone quotes *The Hystorie of Hamblet*, 1608, chap. ii: 'to try if men ... bee extract out of their wits.' Steevens cites the phrase 'extractus a mente' used in the sense of 'insane' by William of Wyrcester, speaking of Henry VI.—**sirrah.** See l. 148, note.

291, 292. **he holds Belzebub at the stave's end:** He makes the fiend keep his distance; defends himself from the attacks of the demon. The figure comes from a duel with staffs—long heavy sticks. Cf. Tilley, *Philological Quarterly*, VI (1927), 310.—**case:** condition.

295, 296. **it skills not much:** it doesn't make much difference.

298. **delivers:** reads the message of.

304. **allow vox:** permit the use of a loud voice—of vociferation.

306–308. **to read his right wits ... thus:** to read in such a way as to express his state of mind correctly is to read as I have already done—with crazy emphasis.—**perpend:** give careful attention.

314–318. **with the which:** i.e., by producing your letter.—**I leave ... injury:** In thus expressing myself I somewhat disregard the respect that is due you and speak as the injury you have done me prompts.

324–327. **so please you ... on't:** If you are willing, after further consideration of what we have just learned, to accept me as a sister-in-law instead of as a wife, the two weddings that shall make me your sister-in-law shall be celebrated on the same day.—**proper:** own.

328. **apt:** ready. Cf. l. 135.

329. **quits you:** releases you from his service.

330. **mettle:** nature, disposition.

337. **Notorious:** notable, egregious.

340. **from it.** *From* is emphatic: 'Write, if you can, in a hand or a style that shall be different from the hand and style shown in this letter.' For *hand* cf. ii, 3, 174, 175. For a similar use of *from* cf. i, 5, 201.

343. **in the modesty of honour:** with some little regard for your own honour.

347. **the lighter people:** 'people of less dignity or importance' (Johnson).

348. **acting . . . hope:** when I acted this part in obedience to your orders and in hope to receive your favour.

351, 352. **geck and gull:** dupe. The words are synonymous. Cf. ii, 5, 204, note.—**play'd on:** made sport with; victimized.

354. **the character:** my handwriting.

355. **out of question:** unquestionably.

358, 359. **presuppos'd Upon thee:** suggested for thy adoption.

360. **This practice . . . upon thee:** This plot has succeeded in working upon thee (in making thee its victim) to the very limit. *Shrewdly* means 'cursedly,' 'confoundedly.'

364, 365. **nor no.** Such double negatives are common. Cf. ii, 5, 203; iii, 1, 171.—**to come:** in the future.—**the condition:** the (happy) nature.

369, 370. **Upon . . . against him:** because of some rude and discourteous acts on his part which had prompted us to feel offended with him.

371, 372. **importance:** importunity; urgent request. Fabian is not quite accurate in saying that Sir Toby urged Maria to write the letter. He obeys his gentlemanly principles by taking the responsibility for the plot upon his own and Sir Toby's shoulders.—**he hath married her.** 'When and where?' the literal-minded chronologists ask. The question is easy to answer:

immediately after Sir Toby has been conducted to bed by Fabian and Feste (l. 215) and at his bedside. Olivia's domestic chaplain was of course instantly available for the ceremony.

373–375. **it was follow'd:** the plan was carried out.—**pluck on:** prompt, induce.—**If that:** if. See i, 2, 48, note.

377. **fool:** dupe.—**baffled thee!** put thee to shame. Cf. ii, 5, 170, note.

380–385. **interlude:** farce.—**that's all one:** that's of no consequence; never mind that.—**Madam, why . . . gagg'd.** See i, 5, 89 ff.—**Thus the whirligig of time brings in his revenges:** Thus time in its whirling course brings with it its appropriate repayments for injuries. That time revolves in a circle is an ancient idea. Cf. *Julius Cæsar*, v, 3, 23–25:

> This day I breathed first. Time is come round,
> And where I did begin, there shall I end.
> My life is run his compass.

387. **notoriously abus'd:** notably (egregiously) ill used. Cf. iv, 2, 95.

390. **the captain.** See ll. 281–283.

391. **convents:** agrees; is convenient.

393. **sister.** Trisyllabic, the final *r* being so pronounced as to count for two syllables. Such a pronunciation sounds odd to-day but was common enough in Shakespeare's time.

396, 397. **habits:** attire. Cf. l. 223; ii, 5, 177; iii, 4, 79.— **mistress:** lady love.—**fancy's:** love's. Cf. i, 1, 14; ii, 4, 34.

398 ff. Editors and critics have vied with each other in denouncing this delightful ditty as nonsensical and un-Shakespearean. Knight goes to the other extreme and describes it as 'the most philosophical Clown's song upon record.' At all events, it is an appropriate ending for a merry play, and I can see no earthly reason for suspecting that it is not Shakespeare's own. However, the reader may take his choice, for the sub-title of the drama is 'What you will'!

398–400. and a. This means merely *a*. *And* is used to carry a note.—**a toy:** a trifle. Cf. iii, 3, 44.

410–412. But ... heads. If this stanza is taken as continuous in sense with the preceding stanza, the meaning may well be: 'I was such a swaggering reveller that I could never prosper, but, whenever I went to bed I always had a drunken head, like other tosspots [i.e., revellers].' As to *had* for 'I had' cf. *has* for 'he has' (i, 5, 156; v, 1, 178, 201, 292). The plurals, *beds* and *heads*, seem to signify the different occasions on which he went to bed drunk. Compare the frequent use of the plural of abstract nouns when two or more persons are referred to. So 'fancies' (ii, 4, 34); 'mercies' (v, 1, 73); 'loves,' 'wisdoms,' 'companies,' 'modesties' (*Hamlet*, i, 1, 173; i, 2, 15; ii, 2, 14, 290), etc. Another possible interpretation of 'When I came unto my bed' is 'when I arrived at the bedtime of life'; 'when I was elderly.' Halliwell (who reads 'bed' and 'head') quotes *Newes* (appended to Overbury's *Characters*, 1615): 'It is said among the folkes heere, that if a man die in his infancy, hee hath only broke his fast [i.e., had breakfast] in this world. If in his youth, hee hath left us at dinner. That it is bedde time with a man at threescore and tenne.' See Rimbault's edition of Overbury, 1856, p. 190. Perhaps *With* is a misprint for *We*. Wilson thinks Feste means 'my wife and I always went drunk to bed together'; but this is to force language unduly.

416. But that's all one: But never mind about that. Cf. ll. 201, 380; i, 5, 137.

417. And we'll strive to please you every day. Such promises from the actors were the regular thing in epilogues. Cf. *Midsummer Night's Dream*, v, 1, 437–445; *All's Well*, v, 3, 335–338; *2 Henry IV*, Epilogue, ll. 27 ff.; *Two Noble Kinsmen*, Epilogue, ll. 15–18.

TEXTUAL NOTES

[Ff indicates the exact agreement of all four Folios—F₁ (1623), F₂ (1632), F₃ (1664), and F₄ (1685). F₁ without mention of the others indicates agreement of the four except in some detail of spelling. The figures 1 and 2 after an editor's name (as in Rowe₁ and Rowe₂) indicate first and second editions. Conjectures are marked 'conj.'; omissions, 'om.']

Act i, Scene 1, 5 sound (Ff)] Wind (Rowe); south (Pope).

11 sea, naught] Sea. Nought (Ff); Sea, Nought (Rowe₂).

23 (stage direction)] After 'her' (l. 23) in Ff; after 'me' (Dyce).

26 heat (F₃ F₄)] heate (F₁ F₂); hence (Rowe₂).

38, 39 fill'd, Her sweet perfections, with (Pope)] fill'd Her sweete perfections with (F₁); fill'd, (O sweet perfection!) with (Warburton); fill'd, (Her sweet perfection) with (Capell).

Scene 2, 10 sav'd (Pope)] saued (F₁); saved (F₂ F₃ F₄).

15 Arion] Orion (Ff); Arion (Pope).

40, 41 company And sight (Hanmer)] sight And company (Ff).

Scene 3, 4 o' (Capell)] a (Ff).

30 almost (Ff)] all, most (Upton conj.; Collier₂).

46 vulgo] vulgo (Ff); volto (Hanmer); Volto (Warburton).

58 And. (F₂ F₃ F₄)] Ma. (F₁).

104 curl by (Theobald)] coole my (F₁).

106 me well (F₂ F₃ F₄)] we wel (F₁).

122 kickshawses] kicke-chawses (F₁ F₂); kick-shawses (F₃); kick-shaws (F₄).

144, 145 flame-colour'd (Rowe₂)] dam'd colour'd (Ff); dun colour'd (Collier MS).

145 stock] stocke (F₁ F₂); stocken (F₃ F₄).

145 set (Rowe₂)] sit (Ff).

148 That's (F₃ F₄)] That (F₁ F₂).

Scene 5, 33 Exit.] om. Ff; Ex. (Pope).

115 Exit Maria.] om. Ff; supplied by Capell.

121 Enter Sir Toby.] After 'comes' in Ff.

129 gentleman here. A] Gentleman heere. A (F₁); Gentleman here. A (F₂ F₃ F₄); Gentleman. Here,—[belches.] A (Theobald); gentleman:—[hiccups.] A (Capell).

146 Exit.] om. Ff; Exit Clown. (Rowe).

176 (stage direction) Viola (F₂ F₃ F₄)] Violenta (F₁).

173

219, 220 Tell . . . messenger.] Continued to Viola in Ff; corrected by Hanmer (Warburton).

236 (stage direction)] om. Ff; supplied by Rowe.

274 with fertile (Pope)] fertill (F₁ F₂ F₃); fertil (F₄).

320 County's] Countes (F₁); Counts (F₂ F₃ F₄); county's (Capell).

Act ii, Scene 1, 17 Messaline (Ff)] Metelin (Hanmer); Mitylene (Capell conj.).

Scene 2, 13, the ring] the Ring (Ff); no ring (Malone conj.; Dyce₂).

21 as (Walker conj., *Shakespeare's Versification*, 1854, p. 279; Dyce₂)] om. F₁; sure (F₂ F₃ F₄).

32 our (F₂ F₃ F₄)] O (F₁).

33 made of, such (Tyrwhitt conj., *Observations and Conjectures*, 1766, p. 45; Rann)] made, if such (Ff); made, e'en such (Capell).

Scene 3, 2 diluculo] *Deliculo* (F₁); *Diliculo* (F₂ F₃ F₄); corrected by Rowe.

9, 10 Does . . . life] Does . . . liues (F₁); Does . . . lives (F₂ F₃ F₄); Does . . . Life (Rowe₂); Do . . . lives (Malone).

27 impeticos (Ff)] impeticoat (Johnson conj.; Steevens 1773).

27 gratillity] gratuity (Johnson conj.; Steevens 1778).

35 give a—(F₃ F₄)] giue a (F₁); give a- (F₂).

52 me, sweet and twenty!] me sweet and twentie: (F₁); me sweet and twenty: (F₂ F₃ F₄); me, Sweet, and twenty: (Theobald); me, sweet, and twenty: (Hanmer); me sweet-and-twenty (Reed 1803).

63 dog] dogge (F₁ F₂); a dog (F₃ F₄).

91 O' (Walker conj., *Critical Examination*, 1860, I, 104; Wilson)] O (Ff).

91 the twelf] the twelfe (F₁ F₂); twelf (F₃ F₄); Twelfth (Rowe); the twelfth (Theobald).

147 a nayword (Rowe)] an ayword (Ff).

165 grounds (F₁)] ground (F₂ F₃ F₄).

184 *And.*] An. (Ff); *Sir Toby.* (Tyrwhitt conj.; **Harness**).

Scene 4, 35 won (Hanmer)] worne (F₁ F₂ F₃); **worn** (F₄).

51 Ay; prithee] I prethee (Ff); Ay; pry'thee (Capell).

54 Fly . . . fly (Rowe)] Fye . . . fie (F₁ F₂); Fie . . . fie (F₃ F₄).

85, 86 lands. . . . her,] lands, . . . her: (F₁); lands, . . . her, (F₂ F₃ F₄); lands; her, (Pope).

91 I (Hanmer)] It (Ff).

102 suffers (Rowe)] suffer (Ff).

106 know—(Rowe)] know. (Ff).

Scene 5, 15 metal (Malone)] Mettle (F₁); Nettle (F₂ F₃ F₄).

39, 43 *Fab.* (Clark and Wright conj.)] *To.* (Ff).

44 the Strachy] the *Strachy* (Ff); the Stratarch (Hanmer conj.); the *Trachy* (i.e., Thrace) (Warburton); Trachyne (Capell conj.); the starchy (i.e., starchery) (Steevens conj.); the Strozzi (Collier conj.); the Tragedy (Bulloch conj., *Studies on the Text of Shakespeare*, 1868, p. 110); the County (Kinnear conj., *Cruces Shakespearianæ*, 1883, p. 168); the Malfi (Elze conj.); the Story (i.e., of the Duchess of Malfy) (Dunlap conj., *Modern Language Notes*, VIII [1893], 127).

66 my—some (Collier)] my some (F₁ F₂); some (F₃ F₄).

70 by th' ears (Hanmer)] with cars (F₁); with cares (F₂ F₃ F₄); with cables (Tyrwhitt conj., *Observations and Conjectures*, p. 27); with cords (Grant White).

90 (stage direction)] om. Ff; *Taking up a Letter.* (Rowe).

125 staniel] stallion (Ff); stanyel (Hanmer).

156 are born (Rowe)] are become (Ff).

157 achieve] atcheeues (F₁); atcheeve (F₂); atchieve (F₃ F₄).

168, 169 thee, 'The Fortunate Unhappy.' Daylight] thee, the fortunate vnhappy [unhappy (F₂ F₃ F₄)] daylight (Ff); thee, The fortunate-unhappy.' Day-light (Capell).

169 champian (F₁ F₂)] champion (F₃ F₄); champaign (Collier₁).

194 dear my (F₃ F₄)] deero my (F₁); deere my (F₂); dear, O my (Daniel conj.; Wilson).

Act iii, Scene 1, 7 king] Kings (F₁); King (F₂ F₃ F₄).

7 lies (Capell)] lyes (Ff); lives (Capell conj.; Steevens 1773).

71 Not (Johnson conj.; Rann)] And (Ff).

75 wise men, folly fall'n, quite taint (Theobald and Tyrwhitt conj.)] wise-mens folly falne, quite taint (F₁); Wise mens folly falne, quite taint (F₂); wise mens folly faln, quite taint (F₃ F₄); wise men, folly-faln, quite taint (Capell); wise men's folly shewn, quite taints (Hanmer).

102 all ready (Malone)] already (F₁ F₂); ready (F₃ F₄).

104 (stage direction)] om. Ff; supplied by Rowe.

123 here (Thirlby conj.; Warburton)] heare (F₁ F₂); hear (F₃ F₄).

133 Hides (Ff)] Hideth (Delius conj.; Globe ed.).

133 heart (F₁)] poore heart (F₂); poor heart (F₃ F₄).

148 me? (Rowe)] me: (Ff).

157, 158 beautiful In .. lip!] beautifull? In ... lip, (F₁ F₂ F₃); beautiful? In ... lip! (F₄); beautiful, In .. Lip! (Rowe).

Scene 2, 10 thee the (F₃ F₄)] the (F₁ F₂).

56 the cubiculo] the Cubiculo (Ff); thy *Cubiculo* (Hanmer); thy cubicle (Wilson).

71 nine (Theobald)] mine (Ff).

Scene 3, 15 And thanks, and ever thanks; and oft good turns (Theobald)] And thankes: and euer oft good turnes (F₁). F₂ F₃ F₄ omit ll. 15, 16.

29 people? (Dyce)] people. (Ff).

Scene 4, 5 Where is (Pope)] Where's (Ff).

15 (stage direction)] om. Ff; supplied by Dyce.

16 The Folios put Malvolio's entrance after 'hither' (l. 15); shifted by Capell.

26 *Oli.*] *Mal.* (F₁); *Ol.* (F₂ F₃ F₄).

54 My (Lettsom conj.; Dyce₂)] Thy (Ff).

76 tang with (F₂ F₃ F₄)] langer with (F₁); tang (Capell).

98 *To.*] om. Ff; *Sir To.* (anon. conj. in Clark and Wright; Wilson).

128 Ay, biddy, (Capell)] I biddy, (Ff); Ay Biddy, (Rowe); Ay biddy, (Pope); Ay, Biddy, (Theobald).

160 Ay, is't, (Collier)] I, ist? (F₁ F₂); I, is't (F₃ F₄); Ay, is't? (Rowe).

188 You ... for't (F₂ F₃ F₄)] Yon ... fot't (F₁).

222 out (Theobald)] on't (Ff).

227 Goes ... grief] Goes ... greefes (F₁ F₂); Goes ... griefs (F₃ F₄); Goes ... Grief (Rowe).

232 honour, sav'd,] honour (sau'd) (F₁); honour (sav'd) (F₂); (honour sav'd) (F₃ F₄); Honour sav'd, (Rowe₁); Honour, sav'd, (Rowe₂).

306 hit (Rowe)] hits (Ff).

368, 369 do, now ... purse? (Dyce and Staunton)] do: now ... purse. (F₁); doe? [do? (F₄)] now ... purse. (F₂ F₃ F₄).

419 *Exit.* (F₂ F₃ F₄)] om. F₁.

428. *Exit.*] om. Ff; *Exit Sir And.* (Theobald).

Aᴄᴛ iv, Scene 1, 24 report—(Staunton)] report, (Ff).

38 stroke (F₁ F₂)] strook (F₃); struck (F₄).

Scene 2, 10 studient] Studient (F₁); Student (F₂ F₃ F₄).

41 clerestories] cleere stores (F₁); cleare stones (F₂); clear stones (F₃ F₄); clear stories (Blakeway conj.; Boswell).

64 soul] soule (F₁); house (F₂ F₃ F₄).

75 to the upshot (Rowe)] the vppeshot (F₁); the upshot (F₂ F₃ F₄).

141 goodman devil] good man diuell (F₁); good man Divell (F₂); good man Devil (F₃ F₄); good Man Drivel (Rowe₂).

Scene 3, 27 jealious] iealious (F₁); jealous (F₂ F₃ F₄).

Aᴄᴛ v, Scene 1, 98 int'rim] *intrim* (F₁); *interim* (F₂ F₃ F₄).
117 hath (Capell)] haue (F₁); have (F₂ F₃ F₄); has (Pope).
134, 136 (stage directions)] om. Ff; supplied by Theobald.
178 Has] H'as (Ff).
206 rogue and a passy measures pavin.] Rogue, and a passy measures panyn: (F₁); Rogue after a passy measures Pavin (F₂ F₃ F₄); rogue, and a past-measure *Painim*. (Pope); rogue and a passy measures paynim; (Grant White₁).
263 preserv'd (F₂ F₃ F₄)] preseru'd (F₁); preferr'd (Theobald).
288 extracting (F₁)] exacting (F₂ F₃ F₄); distracting (Hanmer).
357 mad. Thou] mad; then (Ff); mad; thou (Rann).
410 beds (F₁ F₂ F₃)] Beds (F₄); bed (Hanmer).
412 With (Ff)] We (Pollard conj.).
412 still had (Ff)] I had (Hanmer); still I had (Collier₂).
412 heads (F₂ F₃ F₄)] heades (F₁); head (Hanmer).

GLOSSARIAL INDEX

bespeak, to speak to, address, v, 1, 192

best (you were), it would be best for you, i, 5, 33

betimes, in good season, ii, 3, 2

better (she were), it would be better for her to, ii, 2, 27

bias, tendency, v, 1, 267

bibble babble, foolish chatter, iv, 2, 105

biddy, hen, chicken, iii, 4, 128

bide, wait patiently for, i, 5, 70; endure, ii, 4, 97; submit to, ii, 4, 127

birdbolt, a blunt arrow for shooting birds, i, 5, 98

black and blue, thoroughly, ii, 5, 12

blazon, *n.*, heraldic warrant, i, 5, 312

blent, *p.p.*, blended, i, 5, 257

blood, nature, iii, 4, 391

bloody, bloodthirsty, iii, 4, 242; of bloodshed, iii, 3, 32

blow, to cause to swell, puff up, ii, 5, 48

board, to accost, i, 3, 59

boil'd to death, ii, 5, 4

bonds, iii, 1, 25

bones, bone bobbins, ii, 4, 46

book (without), by heart, i, 3, 28, 29; ii, 3, 160, 161

botch'd up, *p.p.*, clumsily contrived, iv, 1, 60

botcher, a tailor who mends clothing, i, 5, 50

bottom, a ship, v, 1, 60

bound, on my way, iii, 1, 85

bout, an exchange of thrust and parry, iii, 4, 336

bow, to yield, ii, 5, 153

brabble, *n.*, a brawl, v, 1, 68

branch'd, *adj.*, ii, 5, 52

breach, breaking waves, ii, 1, 24

breast, voice, ii, 3, 19

breath, voice, ii, 3, 21, 56

bred, *p.p.*, begotten, i, 2, 22

brock, a badger, ii, 5, 114

broke, *p.p.*, broken, v, 1, 178. *See* head

Brownist, iii, 2, 34

bum-baily, a bailiff, a sheriff's officer, iii, 4, 191

but, but that, i, 5, 295; iii, 1, 44; iv, 3, 15; than, i, 4, 13; merely, i, 5, 272; (that), but for the fact that, v, 1, 32

butt'ry bar, i, 3, 75

by, *adv.*, near by, iv, 3, 24

by-and-by, very soon, iii, 4, 189

by'r Lady, by our Lady (the Virgin), ii, 3, 65

canary, a kind of sweet wine, i, 3, 85

Candy, Candia, Crete, v, 1, 64

canton, a song, i, 5, 289

capacity, receptive power, i, 1, 10; understanding, ii, 5, 128

Capilet, a horse's name, iii, 4, 315

care for, to feel anxiety about, worry about, iii, 1, 30

careful, studious, iv, 2, 12

carpet consideration, iii, 4, 257, 258

carry, to manage, iii, 4, 149

case, *n.*, skin, v, 1, 168; condition, v, 1, 292

Castiliano vulgo, i, 3, 46

Catayan, a native of Cathay (China), ii, 3, 80

catch, a round, ii, 3, 18, 61, 66, 98, 101

celebration, i.e., of marriage, iv, 3, 30

chambermaid, confidential lady-in-waiting, i, 3, 55

champian, champaign, open country, ii, 5, 169

chantry, a chapel, iv, 3, 24

character, handwriting, v, 1, 354; appearance, i, 2, 51

charges, is incumbent on, ii, 1, 14

charity (of), v, 1, 237

check, to fly off, ii, 5, 125; iii, 1, 71

cherry-pit, a childish game, iii, 4, 129

chev'ril, made of cheveril (a kind of kid), iii, 1, 14

choose (can not), cannot help, ii, 5, 192; (shall not), iv, 1, 61

Christian, i, 3, 90

chuck, chick, dear, iii, 4, 126

churchman, an ecclesiastic, a clergyman, iii, 1, 4

circumstance, circumstances, iii, 4, 286

civil, sedate, iii, 4, 5

clause, a proposition, iii, 1, 165

clerestories, iv, 2, 41

clodpoll, a dunce, iii, 4, 210

cloistress, a nun, i, 1, 28

close, in hiding, ii, 5, 21

cloyment, satiety, ii, 4, 102

cockatrice, a basilisk, iii, 4, 215

cockney, a silly creature, iv, 1, 14

codling, an unripe apple, i, 5, 166

coffer, one's store of money, iii, 4, 381

cohere, to coincide, agree, v, 1, 259

cold scent, ii, 5, 133

collier, iii, 4, 130

colours (fear no), i, 5, 6

come (away), *imv.*, come hither, ii, 4, 52; (near me), iii, 4, 71; (thy ways), come on, come along, ii, 5, 1; (to note), to be made public, iv, 3, 29

comedian, an actor, i, 5, 194

comfort, to sustain, iii, 4, 35

commerce, conversation, iii, 4, 189

commission, a message, an errand, i, 5, 201

commodity, a lot, iii, 1, 50

compáct, v, 1, 163

compare, comparison, ii, 4, 104

compass, to bring about, effect, i, 2, 44

competent, sufficient, adequate, iii, 4, 268

competitor, an associate, iv, 2, 12

complexion, temperament, ii, 5, 31

compliment, ceremony, iii, 1, 110

comptible, sensitive, i, 5, 188

con, to study, learn, i, 5, 187; ii, 3, 160

conceited, iii, 4, 322

condition, nature, v, 1, 365

conduct, *n.*, escort, iii, 4, 263

confine, to attire, i, 3, 10

consanguineous, ii, 3, 84

conscience, consciousness, iii, 3, 17; (in my), iii, 1, 32, 33

consequently, as a logical consequence, iii, 4, 77

consideration (carpet), iii, 3, 257, 258

consonancy, consistency, ii, 5, 141

constant, consistent, iv, 2, 53

constellation, i, 4, 35

conster, to construe, interpret, explain, iii, 1, 63

construction, interpretation, ii, 3, 189; judgment, iii, 1, 126

contagious, catchy, ii, 3, 56, 57

contempt of question (in), ii, 5, 97

continent, a container, v, 1, 278

control, authority, ii, 5, 73

convent, to agree, be convenient, v, 1, 391

coranto, a running dance, i, 3, 136

Count (his), County's, Count's, iii, 3, 26

counterfeit, to pretend, iv, 2, 122

country (*trisyllabic*), i, 2, 21

County, Count, i, 5, 320

cousin, niece, i, 3, 5; uncle, i, 5, 131

coxcomb, pate, v, 1, 179, 193, 194; a fool, v, 1, 212

coystril, a groom, a low fellow, i, 3, 44

cozier, a cobbler, ii, 3, 98

credit, belief, iv, 3, 6

Cressida, iii, 1, 58, 62

cross-garter'd, ii, 5, 164

crow, *v.*, i, 5, 94

crowner, a coroner, i, 5, 142

cruelty, a cruel person, i, 5, 307; ii, 4, 83

crush, to use force with, ii, 5, 153

cry upon't, to have a try at it, ii, 5, 135

cubiculo, cubicle, private room, iii, 2, 56

cuckold, the husband of an unfaithful wife, i, 5, 57

cucullus non facit monachum, i, 5, 61, 62

cunning, *n.*, craft, craftiness, ii, 2, 23; (in a), by a trick, iii, 1, 127

cunning, *adj.*, skilful, expert, i, 5, 258; iii, 4, 313

curate, a' parish priest, iv, 2, 2

curst, ill-tempered, cross, iii, 2, 45

Cut, a dock-tailed horse, ii, 3, 202

cypress, a coffin of cypress wood, ii, 4, 53

cypress, a veil of black cyprus (crape), iii, 1, 132

dally, to play, sport, ii, 4, 48; iii, 1, 16

damask, *adj.*, of mingled red and white, ii, 4, 115

dam'd colour'd, i, 3, 144 (note)

dark room, iii, 4, 148

day-bed, a sofa, ii, 5, 54

deadly life, i, 5, 284

dealing, payment, iii, 3, 18

dear, costly, expensive, iii, 2, 58; (*emphasizing*), i, 4, 25; v, 1, 74

deceivable, deceptive, misleading, iv, 3, 21

decreed, *p.p.*, fated, i, 5, 330

dedication, devotion, v, 1, 85

defence, skill in fencing, iii, 4, 240

defy, to renounce, iv, 1, 108

degree, rank, i, 3, 125; iii, 4, 82; a step, iii, 1, 134

deity, divine quality, v, 1, 234

deliver, to report, reveal, i, 2, 42; i, 5, 221; read the message of, v, 1, 298; release, iv, 2, 73

denay, denial, refusal, ii, 4, 127

deny, to refuse, iii, 4, 231; iv, 1, 62; v, 1, 93

desperate assurance, ii, 2, 7

desperate of, in utter disregard of, v, 1, 67

despite, angry defiance, iii, 4, 242

determinate, *adj.*, decided upon, ii, 1, 11

detested, *p.p.*, cast off with a curse, v, 1, 142

detraction, defamatory speech, ii, 5, 150

dexteriously, dextrously, i, 5, 66

diluculo surgere, ii, 3, 2

dimension, figure, form, i, 5, 280; v, 1, 244

discard, to cast off, refuse to associate with, iii, 4, 99

discourse (all), all reason, iv, 3, 12

discover, to disclose, reveal, ii, 5, 169

dishonest, dishonourable, iii, 4, 421; iv, 2, 35; untrustworthy, i, 5, 46

dishonesty, dishonourable character, iii, 4, 422

dismount, to unsheathe, iii, 4, 245

disorders, disorderly conduct, ii, 3, 104

dispatch, management, iv, 3, 18

display'd, *p.p.*, full blown, ii, 4, 40

disposition, frame of mind, iii, 1, 147

dispute, to argue, iv, 3, 9

dissemble, to disguise, iv, 2, 4; conceal one's true character, iv, 2, 5

dissembling, *adj.*, v, 1, 167

distaff, a staff used in spinning, i, 3, 107

distemper, to infect, ii, 1, 4

distemper'd, *adj.*, diseased, i, 5, 97

distract, *adj.*, distracted, v, 1, 287

divinity, sacred discourse, i, 5, 233, 235

divulg'd, publicly reputed, i, 5, 279

dog, an adept, ii, 3, 63

dormouse, *adj.*, sleepy, dormant, iii, 2, 20

phatic), away from, foreign to, i, 5, 201;
differently from, v, 1, 340
fulsome, nauseous, v, 1, 112
function, priestly office, iv, 2, 9; v, 1,
164
fustian, *adj.*, nonsensical, ii, 5, 119

gait, going, steps, i, 4, 15; iii, 1, 93
gall, bitterness, iii, 2, 53
galley, a ship, iii, 3, 26
galliard, a lively dance, i, 3, 127, 136, 143
gaskins, galligaskins, loose breeches, i, 5,
26
geck, a dupe, v, 1, 351
generous, high-minded, i, 5, 97
genius, one's ego, iii, 4, 142
gentleman, an attendant gentleman, v, 1,
184, 186
gentleness, love and favor, ii, 1, 45
gentlewoman, a lady in waiting, i, 5, 173
giddily, slightly, ii, 4, 87
gin, a snare, ii, 5, 92
ginger, ii, 3, 126
give place, to withdraw, depart, ii, 4, 82;
give way, ii, 4, 127
glass, a mirror, iii, 4, 415; a perspective
glass, v, 1, 272
go (even), to be in accord, agree, v, 1, 246;
(to), *interj.*, i, 5, 45; ii, 5, 164; iii, 4,
57, 105; iv, 1, 3; (with), to associate
with, iii, 4, 298
God b' wi' you, good-bye, iv, 2, 108
goes fairly, sounds well, iv, 2, 11
good life, morality, ii, 3, 36, 38
goodman, iv, 2, 141
good my lord, v, 1, 109
goose-pen, iii, 2, 53
Gorboduc, iv, 2, 18
grace, the favour of heaven, iii, 1, 147;
virtue, v, 1, 35; *pl.*, beauties, i, 5, 260
gracious, handsome, i, 5, 281; pleasing,
delightful, ii, 3, 21
grain (in), dyed in fast colours, i, 5, 256
grand-jurymen, iii, 2, 17
gratillity, a little gratuity, ii, 3, 27
gravity, a dignified person, iii, 4, 129
Greek, a nonsensical talker, iv, 1, 19
green, pale and sallow, ii, 4, 116
grize, a step, iii, 1, 135
grizzle, mingled dark and grey hair, v, 1,
168
gross, low, vulgar, ii, 5, 171
grossly, in material substance, v, 1, 244
grossness, obvious impossibility, iii, 2, 78
grounds of faith, fixed belief, ii, 3, 165
guard (out of his), defenceless, i, 5, 92
gull, *n.*, a dupe, iii, 2, 73; v, 1, 214, 351
gull, *v.*, to trick, ii, 3, 147
gull-catcher, ii, 5, 204
gust, taste, fondness, i, 3, 32

ha (*interrogative*), iii, 4, 46; iv, 2, 85
habit (habits), costume, attire, ii, 5, 177;
iii, 4, 79; v, 1, 223, 396
haggard, a wild or untrained hawk, iii, 1,
71
hale, to haul, iii, 2, 64
halt, to limp, v, 1, 195
hand, handwriting, iii, 4, 31; v, 1, 340,
355
hand (by this), an oath, ii, 3, 133
hand (in), to do with, i, 3, 69
haply, perchance, i, 2, 54
happily, haply, perchance, iv, 2, 56
happy, fortunate, ii, 5, 177
has, he has, i, 5, 156; v, 1, 178, 201, 292
have, to find, iii, 3, 42
having (my), *n.*, what I have, iii, 4, 379
haviour, behaviour, iii, 4, 226
head (break), to break the skin of one's
head, v, 1, 178, 188
heart (my profound), i, 5, 195
hearts, *voc.*, fine fellows, ii, 3, 16
heat, course, i, 1, 26
heat (above), i, 5, 140
held out, *p.p.*, maintained, iv, 1, 5
here and everywhere, omnipresence, v, 1,
235
high, in the highest degree, i, 1, 15
his, its, v, 1, 385
hob, nob, iii, 4, 261
hold, to value, ii, 4, 87; contain, ii, 4, 99
hold acquaintance, i, 2, 16
horrible, horribly, iii, 4, 192
house, a room, iv, 2, 44
how now? how d'ye do? i, 3, 48
hull, to lie adrift, i, 5, 217
humour, disposition, ii, 5, 58; a whim, ii,
5, 93; capriciousness, i, 4, 5
hunter, a hound on the trail, iii, 4, 242
hyperbolical, turbulent, raging, iv, 2, 29

idle, foolish, iii, 4, 136; (markets), unnecessary spending, iii, 3, 46
idleness, trivial pastime, i, 5, 70
if that, if, i, 5, 324; v, 1, 375
impeticos, to pocket, ii, 3, 27
importance, importunity, v, 1, 371
in, in the person of, ii, 2, 24
incardinate, incarnate, in the flesh, v, 1,
185
incensement, anger, iii, 4, 259
incredulous, incredible, iii, 4, 89
India, the East Indies, ii, 5, 16
Indies, iii, 2, 84
indifferent, *adv.*, more or less, rather, i, 5,
265; (well), pretty well, well enough,
i, 3, 144
indue, to endow, i, 5, 105
ingrate, ungrateful, thankless, v, 1, 116
ingrateful, ungrateful, v, 1, 80

106
80 r